Independent Reading Activities

That Keep Kids Learning
...While You Teach Small Groups

by Susan Finney

SCHOLASTIC
PROFESSIONAL BOOKS

New York ✦ Toronto ✦ London ✦ Auckland ✦ Sydney
Mexico City ✦ New Delhi ✦ Hong Kong ✦ Buenos Aires

DEDICATION

*To Frances Cordelia, my beautiful first grandchild,
who was wise enough to choose the perfect parents.*

" And pray, and sing, and tell old tales, and laugh at gilded butterflies. "

—King Lear

Cover design by Maria Lilja
Interior design by Grafica, Inc.
Interior photos courtesy of the author

ISBN 0-439-30941-7

TABLE OF CONTENTS

TABLE OF CONTENTS

INTRODUCTION

Effective teachers are always looking for ways to improve their teaching. In fact, one of the best things about teaching is that we are always learning. We learn from the teacher in the classroom next door, we learn from professional publications, and we learn from professional development programs and seminars. To inform ourselves further, we stay abreast of current research through the Internet and we have collegial conversations. In this book you'll find some of the things I've learned about teaching and about reading instruction that I am pleased to share with others.

Below are the three major instructional goals that I hope this book will help you achieve:

1. Use small-group settings to meet differing literacy needs

For a very long time, many of us tried to teach reading as a whole-class activity. It didn't work. And it didn't work because an essential component was missing: We hadn't learned about the children. In Carol Ann Tomlinson's words, "When somebody hands you a glob of kids, they don't hand you a matched set." Until we know about children's differing needs, it's impossible to plan instruction. That is why raising reading achievement is one of the most challenging tasks we face as educators.

In the majority of third- through sixth-grade classrooms across the nation, children are not just reading below grade level, they are reading at many different levels. Because students are not all on the same page, classroom practice must reflect a view of literacy that focuses on maximizing learning for all students. To create an effective reading program, teachers need to provide students with learning opportunities that are at their instructional levels. To do so requires a small-group setting.

2. Offer literacy center activities and long-term projects to provide learning outside the groups

Once students leave the small group, their activities should also be literacy-focused. Outside the group, students should read more, write more about what they're reading, and have more literate conversations with their peers. Outside the group, they should learn to work independently as well as collaboratively, and they should have many heterogeneous learning experiences.

These learning experiences can take many forms. In this book you'll find them grouped into two major categories—activities for the classroom literacy centers and ongoing assignments called "Long-Term Never-Ending Projects." These independent and collaborative learning experiences are designed to build on skills that have been introduced and practiced within the reading groups. Plan to teach the skills, concepts, strategies, and processes as part of your guided-

reading lessons before expecting students to work at them independently. You'll find helpful recommendations and specific "how-to"s about adapting center activities and long-term projects to accommodate individual differences in the introductions to the chapters.

3. Manage small groups and independent activities effectively

For many teachers a move from whole-class reading instruction to small groups creates stressful management and instructional concerns. This book is intended to provide the tools you need to structure literacy-focused activities for the rest of the class so that you can teach small groups. The strategies upon which these activities are based have been used successfully in hundreds of classrooms across the United States and Canada. They reflect not only a strong research base but more than twenty-five years of classroom experience. They will allow you to provide a more enriched curriculum, meet the needs of all of your students and, at the same time, give you easily-implemented and practical management strategies.

This book is intended to be a guide to improving your effectiveness as a teacher of reading. It is also a "how-to" book—how to use your time and your students' time more productively. Finally, it is a resource—a compendium of ideas to support student achievement and maximize learning. Throughout, you will find innovative and practical strategies designed to help you strengthen the reading skills of each of your students and transform your classroom into one where you can really teach.

Susan Finney

CHAPTER 1

Managing a Dynamic Classroom:

Literacy Centers, Independent Work, and Collaborative Activities

I meet teachers every week who are excited about setting up small group instruction in their own classrooms. They know from experience that there is no one-size-fits-all reading program. Many of them, especially the intermediate teachers, confront classrooms with ranges of reading ability that span three or four grade levels. These teachers know that in order for children to benefit from instruction, they must be working with books at their instructional level—books they can read with 90% accuracy. So, these teachers understand that their students cannot all be using the same text. Small, homogeneous groups that are based on instructional levels and needs, with ongoing assessment and potential for movement among the groups, are the answer. That much is clear.

But there are two things that remain of concern: "What is everyone else doing?" and "How can I effectively monitor what they're doing and still focus on teaching my reading group?" The simple, in-a-nutshell answer is that you need to establish a dynamic classroom environment—one that nurtures active learning—as the basis for flexible grouping. That's a start but it still leaves open these key questions:

◆ How can that be accomplished?

◆ What does that classroom look like?

Providing specific answers to these questions is the goal of this book.

To create and maintain classrooms in which students are actively involved in their own learning and make productive use of their time, we need to understand two basic concepts. The first is that it is impossible to teach small groups effectively unless students outside the group are involved in an organizational plan that really works. The classroom must run smoothly. The second thing we must realize is that what "everyone else" is doing provides the underlying structure.

To that end, the research-supported and classroom-tested strategies in this book are designed to:

1. Help you create a learning environment in your classroom based on established routines that promote student independence and interdependence.

2. Emphasize the importance of using well-designed and purposeful literacy activities based on meaningful engagement with both content and skills.

As part of the organizational plan, literacy activities outside the reading group should offer options for heterogeneous grouping and collaborative work. The social interaction that

results makes for thoughtful discussion, problem solving, clarification, thinking out loud and personal connections among children with very different strengths. These experiences should be balanced with activities and projects that nurture independence.

To sum up, when students leave the reading group, there are three primary options. They may:

1. Collaboratively or independently complete after-reading work, which includes follow-up tasks related to the reading lesson.

2. Collaboratively or independently work at literacy centers.

3. Collaboratively or independently work on their long-term never-ending project.

The discussion that follows lays out the basic guidelines for setting up and managing this kind of dynamic classroom. And to best address your questions and concerns, the discussion focuses upon these FAQs—frequently asked questions.

What Are Literacy Centers?

▶▶ Literacy centers are designated places in the classroom that house activities for extension and reinforcement of skills and strategies already taught in the reading group. Students go to these centers to pick up their work, but they may engage in the literacy center activities virtually anywhere (under tables, in quiet corners, outside the door—it's up to you and the space you are teaching in). Students may also work collaboratively with other students. Center activities not only provide wonderful opportunities for children to work heterogeneously, they can also be differentiated to accommodate the varying needs and abilities of each of your students. Since strategy reinforcement is the basis for center work, students already know how to do the activities. This means no interruptions for questions. Holding students accountable for work done at centers is key to their success. You can maintain accountability by incorporating student contracts and strict due dates, and you can monitor the work done at centers easily by having students periodically bring their Centers Folders to the guided reading group.

What Do Literacy Centers Look Like?

➤➤ Simple, very simple. Literacy centers do not even need to take up floor space. For example, take a large sheet of construction paper, fold it in half to make an envelope and staple it to the wall. Put center activities inside, and voila—you've created a center. Or, tape the sides and hang the envelope on a bookcase, a file cabinet, or the back of a chair. Children just need to know where to go to get their work. Any books connected with a center's work can simply be leaning against the wall or on a nearby bookshelf. And once students have picked up their center activity, they may find somewhere comfortable to work—whether it's alone, in pairs, or with a small group.

Why Use Literacy Centers?

➤➤ The primary purpose of literacy centers is to reinforce literacy skills by giving students opportunities to practice strategies they've learned in their guided reading groups. *Avoid "busy work"* by tying all center work to content and skills that are being taught as part of your curriculum. *Avoid boredom* by using a variety of resources at different levels and creating interesting tasks. *Avoid frustration* by clearly stating the purpose of the activity (with the whole class and again, if needed, in the small group), clarifying what students are actually to "do," and by pre-teaching skills and adjusting assignments when necessary. *Incorporate challenge* because real learning takes place when the difficulty level is such that students have to "reach" slightly above their level.

How Can I Differentiate Literacy Center Activities to Meet the Needs of My Multi-Ability Classroom?

➤➤ Determine the skill or concept you want to reinforce, and set up the activity accordingly. Remember, this skill or concept should be one your students have already been taught. In general, the literacy center activities are the same for all students, but assignments can be tiered if you make use of differentiated (or leveled) resources or materials, and if you incorporate choice. Students and teacher together (in the reading group) can decide which questions, and how many questions, are to be answered, and which materials are to be used.

➤➤ You can also achieve differentiation by assigning specific questions that have been adjusted for complexity, learning styles, readiness, and/or interest. I recently worked with a wonderful fifth-grade teacher who wanted nonfiction reading to be a literacy center focus. We provided a menu of varied generic questions based on Bloom's Taxonomy as the literacy center activity. The questions were all open-ended and ranged from lower-level, recall-type questions to more evaluative ones. We put several nonfiction children's magazines on a table. Some were written for children reading at third- and fourth-grade level and some were written for children reading at or above grade level. Students chose the articles they wanted to read and then selected the open-ended questions they wanted to answer.

➤➤ In addition, you can adjust literacy center activities to accommodate students who may need more scaffolding or more time. (Your more able students can continue working on their long-term never-ending projects, while struggling students are given extra time or support to finish center work.)

How Many Literacy Centers Should I Create in My Classroom?

➤ Start with one or two; staying sane is part of this picture. Create literacy center activities that can be used in several different ways or be recycled at a later date. If the center activities are open-ended and students can work anywhere in the classroom, it is conceivable that one-third of your class might be working on the same center activity using different materials at different levels. Plan your center activities so that they cannot be finished quickly. A good center activity should last about two weeks. Once you feel comfortable with two literacy centers, add a third. You shouldn't really need more than that.

When Do Students Work on Literacy Center Tasks?

➤ When students are not in their reading groups for instruction, they may work on literacy center activities, or do after-reading work and/or work on their long-term never-ending project. The guided-reading group management plan (see the example on page 13) suggests a format in which the teacher meets with struggling readers every day, but less frequently with other groups. Time not spent in the reading group is time for literacy center work, projects, and after-reading work.

How Do Students Manage Their Time?

➤ From the beginning you'll need to establish deadlines and lay out clear expectations for behavior. Checklists, contracts, or a daily journal page to record activities are all means by which you can manage and monitor centers. (See page 14 for an example of a student contract.) When adjustments to assignments are made, both teacher and student sign to indicate agreement; this allows students to have some ownership over what is expected of them. The lines at the bottom of the contract

may be used to write out those adjustments, for specific reminders for the student, or simply for your comments following the completion of the contract.

Students need to work consistently on center assignments, after-reading work, and the long-term never-ending projects. The message is that work is never finished. Your challenge is to make it all interesting. The bottom line: *During the literacy time block, all activities focus on literacy.*

What About Accountability? How Are Centers Corrected?

➤ I discovered quite early that a random check of progress was a good idea. This can be done quite easily, when children are with you in their reading groups. Since all center work is kept in a manila folder, you can simply ask children to bring their folders to the reading group. On the day center work is due, you collect the folders. It is essential that students perceive their work at literacy centers as important. The only way that happens is if it impacts the reading grade. Center activities can be graded separately, graded separately but averaged, or graded holistically. (See page 12 for an example of a holistic rubric.)

➤ A few comments about rubrics: The use of rubrics inspires children to reach higher. (I have never had a child tell me that he or she aspired to be a C or a D student!) Essentially, a rubric tells a student what is needed for a particular grade. Knowing what is required ahead of time is the magic of rubrics. Because a student must meet all the criteria in a grade category to earn that grade and because these criteria are presented from the start, students understand the integrity of the rubric system. (And because of that integrity, bear in mind that any pluses or minuses added to grades or changes to the rubric should be clearly explained.)

→ Whatever record-keeping method is used, students should be able to account for time spent each day, as well as for the learning experiences that they've had.

What Does the Classroom Look Like?

→ It's a busy place. Students are motivated because there is freedom of movement and choice of activities. The teacher is actively involved in teaching, not simply assigning and assessing. This is not an autocratic environment, but one in which students develop responsibility for their own learning. Students are engaged and active, and they may be working alone or they may be in small collaborative groups. Because the organizational structure has been taught and practiced, students make meaningful decisions about how they spend their time. They also understand why they are working at a particular literacy center or why a particular long-term project is worthwhile.

What About Logistics and Procedures?

→ Students need to learn organizational skills. Manila folders should hold all work. The folders themselves should be filed alphabetically in file bins or standing holders. One file bin might hold the manila folders for students' center work; another might hold the manila folders accumulating tasks that are part of the long-term never-ending project.

→ Self-monitoring, awareness of time, and attention to deadlines are essential. When a reading group is meeting with the teacher, the question the other students should ask is: "What can I be doing now?" When the group leaves the teacher, the question should be: "What else do I need to do?" Teach your students that transitions can be signals for self-monitoring.

→ The contract is the keystone to the structure. In very simple terms, it spells out what is expected. Its effectiveness will be reflected in the behaviors seen in your classroom.

→ Students receive the contract every two weeks, as literacy center activities should, ideally, be designed to last that long. (Use the examples in this book as a springboard for your own ideas as well, to aid in creating in-depth literacy center activities and assignments, each with multiple tasks. The last thing you want are center activities that are quickly finished!)

→ When the two weeks are over, collect the literacy center activities folders (you'll need one for the center activities and another for the long-term never-ending projects) and grade them. Some teachers prefer to grade the activities holistically, others grade each individual center activity. Either way, literacy center activities should be considered a part of the total reading grade.

→ Grades for the long-term never-ending projects (which actually do end after about four to six weeks) also influence the total reading grade. Grading criteria should include evidence of thoughtful work, completeness, neatness, and presentation. To maintain accountability, ask students periodically to being their project folders to the reading group where you can check progress.

→ The infrastructure of a guided-reading classroom is based on student routines, record keeping, and time management. The infrastructure, however, is just the means to an end. Without it, one cannot teach small groups.

—In the words of Richard Allington
(What Really Matters for Struggling Readers, 2001):

" *Classroom teachers need time to teach. They need uninterrupted time to teach. Kids need time to learn. To read. To write. Uninterrupted learning time.* "

It's all about time. Now is the time. This book will get you started.

Centers Rubric

Name: _____

Date Started: _____ **Date Completed:** _____

4 _____ of the required _____ activities were completed on time.

The directions were followed for each activity.
All center work was responsibly kept in the Centers Folder.
All work was neat and complete.
The checklist or menu accurately reflected excellent student accountability.
Collaborative and independent behavior at centers was exemplary.

3 _____ of the required _____ activities were completed on time.

Most of the directions were followed for each activity.
All center work was responsibly kept in the Centers Folder.
Most work was neat and complete.
The checklist or menu accurately reflected good student accountability.
Collaborative and independent behavior at centers was very good.

2 _____ of the required _____ activities were completed on time.

Some of the directions were followed for each activity.
Some center work was kept in the Centers Folder.
Some work was neat and complete.
The checklist reflected some sense of accountability.
Collaborative and independent behavior at centers was fair.

1 _____ of the required _____ activities were completed on time.

Few directions were followed.
Little of the center work was kept in the Centers Folder.
Little effort was made to be neat or to complete work.
The checklist showed very little sense of accountability.
Collaborative and independent behavior at centers was poor.

Guided Reading Groups: A Plan For Making Them Work and Keeping Them Flexible

MONDAY	TUESDAY	WEDNESDAY	THURSDAY	FRIDAY
Rats on the Roof (Group A—25 min.)	*Amber Brown Is Not a Crayon* (Group B—20 min.)	*Because of Winn-Dixie* (Group C—20 min.)	*Amber Brown Is Not a Crayon* (Group B—20 min.)	*Rats on the Roof* (Group A—25 min.)
Amber Brown Is Not a Crayon (Group B—20 min.)	*Rats on the Roof* (Group A—25 min.)	*Dominic* (Group D—20 min.)	*Rats on the Roof* (Group A—25 min.)	*Amber Brown Is Not a Crayon* (Group B—20 min.)
Dominic (Group D—20 min.)	*Because of Winn-Dixie* (Group C—20 min.)	*Rats on the Roof* (Group A—25 min.)	*Because of Winn-Dixie* (Group C—20 min.)	*Dominic* (Group D—20 min.)

Group A

Meet with these struggling readers every day and add in extra time for supplementary skill work and reading instruction. (*Rats on the Roof*, by James Marshall, has a R.L. of 2.5.)

Group B

These students are reading below grade level but are showing steady improvement. Meet with them four days a week. (*Amber Brown Is Not a Crayon*, by Paula Danziger, has a R.L. of 3.0.)

Group C

This third group reads at grade level or slightly above. Meet with them three days a week, as they are able to work independently and demonstrate accountability. (*Because of Winn-Dixie*, by Kate DiCamillo, has a R.L. of 4.0.)

Group D

Reading above grade level, these students should be challenged with choice menus. Raise the bar! Require independence as well as collaboration. Adjust the plan— meet with them just once or twice a week. (*Dominic*, by William Steig, has a R.L. of 6.0.)

Independent Reading Activities That Keep Kids Learning...While You Teach Small Groups • Scholastic Professional Books

Student Contract for Literacy Center Activities

Name: _____

Date: _____ **Date Due:** _____

Directions: This is a two-week contract. Staple or glue it to the cover of a manila folder. Use it to keep track of the days when you work on literacy center activities. You are required to work on them at least three days a week. Keep all your work in your Centers Folder. When you have finished an activity, put a 4 in the last column. Bring this folder to your reading group.

CENTER #	M	T	W	TH	F	M	T	W	TH	F	WHEN FINISHED

For this contract,

_____

_____

_____

_____

_____   _____
STUDENT SIGNATURE   **TEACHER SIGNATURE**

Independent Reading Activities That Keep Kids Learning... While You Teach Small Groups • Scholastic Professional Books

CHAPTER 2

Choice Menus and Adjusted Questions:

Practical Strategies for Addressing Differing Needs in Literacy Centers

When students leave the reading group and begin assigned center activities, you have two valuable instructional and management options available for differentiating student work: choice menus and adjusted questions. Whether you offer these strategies to students as they work independently or in small heterogeneous groups, you will be able to address the needs of your varied learners without having to create separate lessons for each child in the classroom. And being able to choose motivates students to learn.

"Choice is motivating because it affords students control. Children seek to be in command of their environment, rather than being manipulated by powerful others. This need for self-direction can be met in reading instruction through well-designed choices." (Guthrie, 2001).

Guthrie also points out that while the experience of making choices is necessary for students to build autonomy, it is the teacher's responsibility to establish the overall sets of texts and tasks from which students make their choices. This is the only way you can be certain that learning and knowledge goals are met.*

Although reading groups are flexible, they are basically homogenous. Children are reading in books that they *can* read. Centers, however, tend to be heterogeneous. When students move from reading groups to centers, you can help them find the right level of challenge by carefully designing choice menus. Such menus, also known as tiered projects, offer differentiated learning experiences. You can adjust questions within choice menus for varying degrees of readiness, depth and complexity, as well as for learning style and preferred intelligence modality.

This chapter provides the following teaching recommendations and student activities to help you establish centers that address your students' varied learning needs, abilities, and goals:

PAGE 18 **Rubric for Choice Menus** offers students a self-evaluation tool that can be applied to any choice menu. The rubric includes both a numbered grading aspect as well as an open-ended "Comments" section. Encourage students to keep a blank copy of the form in each choice menu folder.

PAGE 19 **A Choice Menu:** *The Littles* is based on a long-time favorite. A transitional chapter book and one of a series, the story is well suited for young chapter book readers as well as for older struggling readers. Together with the teacher, students decide which activities will be completed based on interest in the task, readiness, and the degree of complexity. For example, a fluent third-grade reader would eagerly explain how the machine worked that lowered the Littles to the kitchen. A struggling fourth grade reader might

focus on more literal questions, such as what the Newcombs planned for their vacation.

PAGE 20 **A Choice Menu:** *The Dragons Are Singing Tonight* is based on a wonderful Jack Prelutsky book of poetry with fabulous illustrations by Peter Sis. For older students whose reading is fluent, a choice menu such as this one may encourage children to work together yet still choose different tasks. Good literate conversation is the most likely result. The vocabulary in the book is challenging, but the questions are adjusted for difficulty.

PAGE 21 **Check Your Choices** provides students with an open-ended choice menu. You can further differentiate and extend this choice menu by featuring books at different levels from which students can choose. Certain books may be designated for specific children or groups.

PAGE 22 **Take Two: An Author Study,** a multi-purpose activity, can be adapted for use within a reading group or as a center. When used within a reading group, it can be used to guide reading discussions and written work for chapter books. Outside the group, as a center activity, it is suitable for both independent or collaborative work and is best applied to picture books rather than chapter books.

PAGE 23 **Poems: Pick Six** incorporates both choice and open-endedness. Be sure to provide poems and poetry books that range from the uncomplicated to the complex. For example, Jack Prelutsky's poems are humorous, but may have difficult vocabulary for some children. The poetry of Douglas Florian spans more readability levels and has wonderful wordplay. Kristine O'Connell George's lovely haiku-type poetry celebrates nature in ways children will appreciate.

PAGE 25 **Poets and Poetry to Share With Children** is addressed to the teacher. It provides a brief bibliography of recommended titles,

---

* Guthrie, J.T. (2001, March). Contexts for engagement and motivation in reading. Reading Online, 4(8).

anthologists, and poets. It is meant only as a springboard, as many of these authors have written or compiled additional captivating books of poetry.

PAGE 26 **Give Me Five!**—one of my all-time favorite choice menus—is completely open-ended. Be sure to use engaging picture books at this center in order to make the decision-making difficult and the conversation interesting. This center will definitely be long-term; the questions require thoughtful answers.

PAGE 27 **Take Two: Comparing and Contrasting Picture Books** is designed to be used at a center composed of Caldecott books or picture books nominated for Young Reader Medals. It requires careful direction and pre-teaching of skills. Offer models or examples that illustrate "good" answers. Designate specific activities for struggling readers to choose from, perhaps fewer than five. Be sure to provide enough guidance so that all students can do this activity independently.

PAGE 28 **Magazine Miscellany** provides nonfiction reading opportunities based on articles in children's magazines (e.g. *Ranger Rick*, *Zoo Nooz*, *Sports Illustrated for Kids*, *TIME for Kids*, *Cobblestone*). It is open-ended; most of the tasks are geared toward the creation of some kind of student product, such as acrostic puzzles, "cloze" sentences, or vocabulary cards. Differentiating the kind of product students create is another way of accommodating learning preferences.

Another way to adjust for student differences is to vary the number of tasks required. This page is an example of that: Some students can be expected to do one task, while others will retain the task menu for subsequent magazine reading and analysis.

The first task asks students to complete an Anticipation Guide. (A reproducible template of

> *When used by the teacher, an Anticipation Guide is an excellent way to build interest in a topic or to introduce the whole class to a new unit of study.*

an Anticipation Guide is on page 29.) This is a student-generated activity. The student's task is to read the article and create ten statements about it that are either true or *deliberately* false. The student then asks a friend to read the statements and indicate agreement, disagreement, or uncertainty by checking "True," "False," or "I Don't Know" in the columns on the left. Finally, both children read the article together and mark "True" or "False" in the columns on the right.

PAGE 30 **Creating Scenes With Words and Pictures** establishes a collaborative learning situation that requires literary discussion. The first four questions are general questions about the scenes depicted in a picture book. The last five questions are far more specific, focusing readers' attention on one particular scene. To differentiate for varying student ability, adjust the number and type of questions to be answered.

Rubric for Choice Menus

Name: _____

Date Started: _____ **Date Completed:** _____

Book Title: _____

Author: _____

Directions: Read this rubric before beginning the choice menu. Attach the choice menu to the inside of a manila folder. Keep your work in the folder and include this page, too.

4
Eight or more questions have been answered completely.

All spelling is proofread and corrected.

Answers are thoughtful and well written.

Answers are appropriately numbered with no more than two answers to a page.

The title page is visually attractive and complete.

All pages are in order and the finished product is clean and neat.

3
Six or more questions have been answered completely.

Most spelling is proofread and corrected.

Answers are thoughtful and well written.

Answers are appropriately numbered with no more than two answers to a page.

The title page is visually attractive and complete.

The finished product is neat.

2
Four or more questions have been answered completely.

Some spelling may not be proofread or corrected.

Most answers are numbered with no more than two answers to a page.

The title page is incomplete or in rough draft format.

Many pages have not been "cleaned up" and may still require rewriting.

1
Two or more questions have been answered completely.

Most spelling is not proofread or corrected.

Answers are incomplete.

The title page is incomplete or missing.

Work is in sloppy or messy condition.

Grade: _____ **Comments:** _____

_____

_____

Independent Reading Activities That Keep Kids Learning... While You Teach Small Groups • Scholastic Professional Books

A Choice Menu: The Littles by John Peterson

Name: _____

Date: _____

Directions: Choose _____ question(s) from each row. On a separate sheet of paper, write the number of each question you selected and answer that question. Attach your answer sheet to this page.

1. Make a list of all the Littles.	**2.** Name ten items smaller than Mr. Little.	**3.** How did the Littles solve the problem with the cat?	**4.** What did Mr. and Mrs. Newcomb plan to do for their vacation?
5. List five reasons why being six inches tall would be good, or advantageous.	**6.** List five reasons why being six inches tall would be a disadvantage.	**7.** Write the word "Littles" the way it's written in this box. Use each first letter to start a phrase or sentence that tells about this tiny family.	**8.** If you could be one of the Littles, who would you be and why?
9. Use one-inch graph paper and show the heights of each member of the Little family. Be sure to label your graph.	**10.** Explain how the machine worked that got the Littles down to the kitchen.	**11.** How did the Littles and the Biggs help each other? List at least three ways.	**12.** Design some ways that the Littles could use some of the appliances in your home.
13. Make up a title for each of the book's eleven chapters.	**14.** Using a large sheet of construction paper and some one-inch graph paper, design a floor plan and some furniture for the Littles.	**15.** What do you own that the Littles would find useful? Make a list. Describe why each item would be helpful.	**16.** Write another chapter for the story, explaining how the Littles convinced the Biggs to keep the cat.

Independent Reading Activities That Keep Kids Learning... While You Teach Small Groups • Scholastic Professional Books

A Choice Menu: The Dragons Are Singing Tonight
by Jack Prelutsky

Name: _____

Date: _____

Directions: Choose eight of these questions to answer. On a separate sheet of paper, write the number of each question you selected and answer that question. Attach your answer sheet to this page.

1. Read the titles of the poems in the Table of Contents. Find four adjectives that are used to describe dragons.	**2.** Jack Prelutsky uses many *sesquipedalian* words (long words with many syllables). List at least twenty.	**3.** Define ten of the words you found in Question 2. Write the line of poetry in which the word appears and replace the word with its definition.	**4.** Make a list of twenty rhyming pairs (e.g., scales -*nails*).
5. Which poem is your favorite? Give four reasons why. Use complete sentences.	**6.** Which poem seems happiest to you? Which one seems saddest? Explain, using complete sentences.	**7.** How did you feel when you read "I Am My Master's Dragon"? What do you think Jack Prelutsky was saying in this poem?	**8.** The poem, "I Am Boom," can be read aloud as a choral reading. Work with two or three friends to perform this poem.
9. Each of the poems tells a story. In a paragraph, summarize one of the stories.	**10.** Explain both the positive and negative aspects of owning a dragon.	**11.** Who is Jack Prelutsky? Who is Peter Sis? (Check the last page of the book.) Write four factual sentences (in your own words, of course) about each of them.	**12.** Research the topic of dragons on the Internet or in an encyclopedia. Categorize the different kinds of dragons.
13. Create a chart that shows the point of view of the narrator in each of the poems.	**14.** Use any of the poems as a model to write a "copycat" poem (a poem in the same style). Write about something you know a lot about.	**15.** Choose a poem and create your own illustration for it.	**16.** Write about the rhyming patterns that Jack Prelutsky uses.

Check Your Choices

Name: _____ **Date:** _____

Directions: Choose one of the books at this center. Write the book's title on a separate answer sheet. After you have read the book, check eight questions below, write the number of each question on your answer sheet, and answer the question in complete sentences next to the number. Attach your answer sheet to this page.

☐ **1.** Does this story remind you of any other story you've read or heard? Which one? What made you think of it?	☐ **2.** What were you wondering about while you read this story?	☐ **3.** What characters were in this story? Which character do you think was the most important? Why?
☐ **4.** What didn't you understand when you were reading this story? What questions do you have?	☐ **5.** In what parts of the story were you able to really picture the events in your head?	☐ **6.** What was the "hook" that made you choose this book? How did the author continue to hold your interest in the story?
☐ **7.** Have you had an experience similar to one you read about in this book? Write about it.	☐ **8.** Why is this a good story? Give five good reasons.	☐ **9.** Summarize the story in a five-sentence paragraph.
☐ **10.** Was there something special about this author's writing that you liked? Describe it.	☐ **11.** Did you know how the story was going to end? At what point did you realize it? What do you think of the ending?	☐ **12.** Would you read another book by this author? Why?

Independent Reading Activities That Keep Kids Learning… While You Teach Small Groups • Scholastic Professional Books

Take Two: An Author Study

Name: _____ **Date:** _____

Directions: For this author study, you will be reading two books by the same author. The choice menu below offers several options for comparing and contrasting the books. Read through the questions before you begin reading the books so that you can be thinking about them as you read. Then, check a minimum of six questions and write the number of each question and your answers on a separate sheet. Attach the sheet to this page.

1. What genre is the first book? What genre is the second book? Explain some of the characteristics of each genre.

2. How would you describe the main characters in each of the books? Write a paragraph about each of them. Use character trait words, such as "shy" or "lazy."

3. With which protagonist (main character) did you identify more? Have similar things happened to you? What do you have in common with that character?

4. Authors do many things to make their characters interesting to readers. How did the author make the main characters in your books interesting?

5. If you were telling someone something important about each of these books, what would you say?

6. How is the setting of the first book different from the setting of the second book? In what ways did that affect the stories?

7. How would you compare the opening and closing scenes in each of the books?

8. How would you compare the conflict or problem that the main characters faced in each book?

9. What literary devices—foreshadowing, irony, humor, simile, metaphor, and so on—did the author use frequently? In which book were they more effective?

10. How would you describe the major differences between the two books?

11. Of the two books, which one did you prefer? Give several reasons.

12. What was the author's purpose in writing these books? Share your thoughts about what the author was trying to accomplish in each of the books.

13. Describe one or two scenes in each of the books that were easy for you to visualize. What made them so real for you?

14. What is the protagonist's goal in each of the books—that is, what did the protagonist want to accomplish?

15. After reading two books by this author, would you read a third? Why?

Independent Reading Activities That Keep Kids Learning... While You Teach Small Groups • Scholastic Professional Books

STUDENT PAGE

Poems: Pick Six

Name: _____ **Date:** _____

Directions: There are several poems and poetry books at this center. Spend some time reading and enjoying the poetry. Pick six poems that you really like and rank them from 1 to 6, giving a 6 to the poem you liked best. Write the titles, the poets' names, and describe something you noticed about each of the poems. (Don't forget to put quotation marks around the titles of the poems.)

Share your poems with three other students. Explain to them why you ranked the poems the way you did. In the "Your Comments" section on the next page, write about what you discovered when you shared your favorites. (Note: Three other students must also share their poems with you.)

Title:	Poet:

What I noticed: _____
_____
_____ **My ranking of this poem:** _____

Title:	Poet:

What I noticed: _____
_____
_____ **My ranking of this poem:** _____

Title:	Poet:

What I noticed: _____
_____
_____ **My ranking of this poem:** _____

Title:	Poet:

What I noticed: _____
_____
_____ **My ranking of this poem:** _____

Independent Reading Activities That Keep Kids Learning... While You Teach Small Groups • Scholastic Professional Books

23

Title:	Poet:

What I noticed: _____

_____

_____ **My ranking of this poem:** _____

Title:	Poet:

What I noticed: _____

_____

_____ **My ranking of this poem:** _____

Your Comments: Answer the following questions in detail and in paragraph form. Make your answers specific by referring *by name* to the students who listened to the poems and to your rankings. There will not be enough room on this page for your answers, so attach additional pages as needed.

◆ What was the most important thing you noticed about the poems you liked?

◆ What did you notice about the poems your friends chose?

◆ What did your friends notice about your poems that you did <u>not</u> notice?

◆ Do you have favorite poets? What are the names of those poets? What are the names of your friends' favorite poets?

◆ Is there a poet you don't like? Who? Why?

◆ Find another poem by one of the poets you liked. Copy it and attach it to this center assignment on a separate page.

_____

_____

_____

_____

_____

_____

_____

_____

Independent Reading Activities That Keep Kids Learning... While You Teach Small Groups • Scholastic Professional Books

Poets and Poetry to Share With Children

Many of the poets and anthologists cited below have produced other wonderful titles that are also worth pursuing. Try to keep a number of these poets' works available at all times in your classroom.

Poet (or Anthologist)	Title
Bouchard, David	Voices from the Wild
Bryan, Ashley	Sing to the Sun
Clinton, Catherine	I, Too, Sing America: Three Centuries of African American Poetry
Esbensen, Barbara	Dance With Me
Fleischman, Paul	Big Talk
Florian, Douglas	Beast Feast
George, Kristine O'Connell	The Great Frog Race
Gollub, Matthew	Cool Melons—Turn to Frogs! The Life and Poems of Issa
Greenberg, Jan	Heart to Heart: New Poems Inspired by Twentieth-Century Art
Grimes, Nikki	It's Raining Laughter
Hopkins, Lee Bennett	Climb Into My Lap
Hopkins, Lee Bennett	My America: A Poetry Atlas of the United States
Janeczko, Paul	A Poke in the I
Johnson, Angela	The Other Side
Larrick, Nancy	Cats are Cats
Larrick, Nancy	Piping Down the Valleys Wild
Levy, Constance	A Crack in the Clouds
Livingston, Myra Cohn	Call Down the Moon
Livingston, Myra Cohn	Roll Along: Poems on Wheels
Nye, Naomi Shihab	The Space Between Our Footsteps: Poems and Paintings from the Middle East
Philip, Neil	Earth Always Endures: Native American Poems
Prelutsky, Jack	The 20th Century Children's Poetry Treasury
Smith, Charles R.	Rimshots: Basketball Pix, Rolls, and Rhythms
Sneve, Virginia Driving Hawk	Dancing Teepees
Wilbur, Richard	The Disappearing Alphabet
Wood, Nancy	Spirit Walker

Independent Reading Activities That Keep Kids Learning… While You Teach Small Groups • Scholastic Professional Books

Give Me Five!

Name: _____ **Date:** _____

Other Group Members: _____

_____

Directions: There are several books at this center. Your assignment is to work with a small group of students and together choose five books that you all like. Then, work together to rate them from 1 to 5. The book your group likes the most should get a 5, the next one a 4, and so on. Show the rating by circling the number below the title. *Each book should have a different rating.* Answer the questions below on another sheet of paper. Respond thoughtfully and in complete sentences. Attach your answer sheet to this page.

Title: _____

1   2   3   4   5

Title: _____

1   2   3   4   5

Title: _____

1   2   3   4   5

Title: _____

1   2   3   4   5

Title: _____

1   2   3   4   5

Questions

1. What is the biggest difference between the two books you all ranked #5 and #1?

2. Who are the main characters in <u>each</u> of the books?

3. Which main character did you like the best? Why?

4. How did your ratings change as you discussed the books?

5. Which book made you think the most? How did the author do that?

6. Which book has the best illustrations? What did the illustrator do?

7. How important are the illustrations to the book you rated #1?

8. What was the hardest ranking decision? What made it difficult to come to agreement?

Take Two: Comparing and Contrasting Picture Books

Name: _____ **Date:** _____

Directions: Read any <u>two</u> of the picture books at this center, then choose <u>five</u> of the ten questions below to answer. You will be comparing and contrasting the two books. Circle the numbers of the questions you choose and write those numbers on a separate sheet of paper. Write your answers on that sheet. Attach it to this page.

1. Describe the main characters in each of the books.

2. Pretend that a younger reader has asked you what the story in each of these books is about. Summarize each book for that child.

3. Describe five major differences between the two books.

4. Use a Venn Diagram to compare the protagonists (main characters) in each of the books.

5. In which book did the author do a better job of holding your interest? Describe what he or she did to hold your interest.

6. In what ways are these books suited to a reader your age? In what ways are they not appropriate?

7. The protagonist in each of the books had a problem to solve. What were the problems and how were they solved?

8. Compare the illustrations in the books. Which do you prefer? If you had created them, what would you have done differently?

9. Why did the authors write these books? Is there a lesson to learn? What is the point? What were they trying to say to their readers?

10. Look for examples of "cause and effect" in each of the two stories. Describe how the authors of each book used "cause and effect" to help tell their stories.

Independent Reading Activities That Keep Kids Learning... While You Teach Small Groups • Scholastic Professional Books

Magazine Miscellany

Name: _____ **Date:** _____

Directions: The magazines at this center all have interesting articles full of information on many different topics. Find an article that interests you and read it. When you have finished the article, write the name of the magazine and the title of the article below. (Don't forget to put quotation marks around the title of the article.) Choose one of the activities listed. Make an X through the box when that activity is completed. Save this page for more magazine reading.

Name of Magazine: _____

Title of Article: _____

Using the form on the next page, create an Anticipation Guide. Make up 10 statements that are "true" or "false" and write them on the form. Give it to a student who hasn't read the article, and have the student respond to the statements. Then, read the article together and complete the Guide.	Read the article and make up three "why" questions, three "where" questions, and three "what" questions. Answer your own questions.	Write ten questions about the article. Write the answers to the questions on index cards and give the cards to another student. Ask the student to read each answer out loud. Have the class try to come up with the appropriate question that goes with each answer.
Go to the library to find more information about the topic of the article you read. Create two clusters—one to show facts from the first article, the second to show the additional information.	What vocabulary was new or interesting in this article? Use an index card for each word and write its definition on the back of the card. Write an original sentence for each word. (minimum: ten words)	Use the title of the article to write an acrostic puzzle summarizing the information in the article. (An acrostic puzzle spells the title in a vertical format.)
Create "cloze" sentences. Write fifteen sentences about the article, leaving an important word out in each sentence. Put a line where the word would be. Provide a word bank so a classmate can "fill in the blanks."	How has the author of this article used language? Are metaphors or similes used to help the reader picture scenes or events? What literary devices did you notice? Share the author's descriptive language.	What kind of article is it? ✦ cause and effect? ✦ problem and solution? ✦ question and answer? ✦ compare and contrast? ✦ descriptive? ✦ other? What makes you think so?

28

Anticipation Guide for

Article Title: _____

Name: _____ **Date:** _____

Name of Student I Worked With: _____

Directions: Use this Guide with the first activity on page 28.

BEFORE READING			STATEMENTS	AFTER READING	
Yes, I agree.	No, I do not agree.	I don't know.		Yes, this is true.	No, this isn't true.
☐	☐	☐		☐	☐
☐	☐	☐		☐	☐
☐	☐	☐		☐	☐
☐	☐	☐		☐	☐
☐	☐	☐		☐	☐
☐	☐	☐		☐	☐
☐	☐	☐		☐	☐
☐	☐	☐		☐	☐
☐	☐	☐		☐	☐
☐	☐	☐		☐	☐

Independent Reading Activities That Keep Kids Learning… While You Teach Small Groups • Scholastic Professional Books

Creating Scenes With Words and Pictures

Name: _____ **Date:** _____

Student(s) I Worked With: _____

Book Title: _____

Author: _____

The setting of a story may be a deep, dark forest, while a *scene* in that story might be the wolf jumping out at the pig. Authors use scenes to show action happening and to move a story forward. By changing the scene (or the action), an author can do several things: For example, he or she can show the problems of the book's characters, make us aware that time has passed, or set the stage for other characters to appear. Authors create scenes with words; illustrators create scenes with pictures. In a picture book, the illustrator creates the scene that the author has described with words.

Directions: Work with a partner or in a small group to discuss and work out a response to each question. Then, after your discussion, write your answers on a separate sheet of paper and attach it to this page.

1. Look at the cover of one of the picture books at this center. What scene has the illustrator depicted? Describe it.

2. As you read the book, notice the different scenes that take place. How many different scenes are there in this story?

3. Pay careful attention to the way the scenes help tell the story. How important are the scenes? Are there some scenes that are not important? Are there scenes that seem to be missing—scenes you might have included if you had written this book?

4. How important are the pictures in showing what is happening in each scene? Do you think the illustrator does a good job in helping tell this story? Why or why not?

Next, choose <u>one</u> scene from your book and answer Questions 5–9 about that scene.

5. What is the main action in the scene you've chosen?

6. Why did the author include this scene?

7. What is the conflict or problem in the scene?

8. Was the problem or conflict resolved? If so, describe how.

9. How is the scene important to the main character?

CHAPTER 3

Picture Books for Older Readers

Why is it that in many intermediate classrooms there are no picture books to be seen? Perhaps it is the rush to transition to chapter books. Perhaps it's that we haven't really considered why picture books should still be part of our literacy curriculum. One of the best sixth grade teachers I've ever known shares her perspective on using picture books with older students: *"In my classroom, Friday is Picture Book Day. The rest of the week, I read aloud from my favorite novels, but I have discovered something I can't ignore—picture books are a powerful teaching tool. I can teach the elements of a plot and introduce literary devices. We can talk about genres. My students have a better conceptual understanding of what a theme is. They pay attention to the interdependence of the illustrations and the text. The whole class can be engaged and focused, and the best part is that their knowledge transfers to their discussions about other literature."*

This chapter offers more than a dozen center activity ideas, as well as several informational pages for teachers that focus on high-quality picture books for readers in the intermediate grades.

PAGE 33 **Conflict Holds a Story Together** combines picture books with activities that are conceptually sophisticated, requiring students to identify the conflict in ten different picture books. Some thought-provoking books you might feature at this center include *Golem* (Wisniewski), *Jumanji* (Van Allsburg), *The Wall* (Bunting), *The Faithful Elephants* (Tsuchiya), *Rose Blanche* (Innocenti), *Fly Away Home* (Bunting), *Raising Dragons* (Nolen), *Oregon's Journey* (Rascal), as well as most of the picture books of Patricia Polacco and William Steig.

PAGE 35 **It Depends on Your Point of View** directs students to focus on *who* is telling the story and asks them to make a personal connection to the text in an extension writing activity.

PAGE 36 **Show What You Know** is an opportunity for students to apply knowledge about genre, point of view, and conflict. Point of view and conflict are discussed in the first two activities in this chapter; genre is covered in Chapter 4. I also offer a detailed discussion of genre in my book, *Keep the Rest of the Class Reading and Writing While You Teach Small Groups* (Scholastic, 2000).

PAGE 37 **The Good Guys and the Bad Guys** invites students to work independently or collaboratively as they determine who the protagonists and the antagonists are in five different picture books. Students must then come up with one question for a protagonist and one for an antagonist.

PAGE 38 **A Choice Menu: *The Secret Knowledge of Grownups*** is based on the very funny book by David Wisniewski. In the book, along with his wonderful trademark paper-cut illustrations, Wisniewski has concocted bizarre reasons why grown-ups have perpetrated certain rules for children. The choice menu, which consists of primarily literal questions, requires students to read a great deal of text very carefully.

PAGE 39 **Theme Talk** challenges students to construct well-crafted sentences that summarize a book's story and theme. Students must use specific vocabulary and a specific number of words in their sentences.

PAGE 40 **Multiple Perspectives and Thought-Provoking Stories: Five Easy Centers,** addressed to the teacher, is an in-depth look at the work of four author/illustrators whose books must be read thoughtfully and strategically. The informational pages about the authors and their books are followed by five center ideas that ask students to compare thematically-related books and to hypothesize, synthesize and evaluate.

PAGE 43 **Thought-Provoking Picture Books** can be used on its own or as an extension of the five "Multiple Perspectives" center ideas (see p. 40). The purpose of the activity is to have students synthesize discoveries about thought-provoking picture books and to provide independent practice in meaningful thinking about their reading.

PAGE 44 **Exploration With a Partner: *Black and White*** is based on a terrific book by David Macaulay. This center is a collaborative post-reading activity that incorporates vocabulary work, planned collaboration and application tasks. While this page is specific to Macaulay's book, the form of questioning demonstrates the more general goal of moving students' reading and thinking from a focus on literal details to concepts that are more abstract.

PAGE 45 **Story Charts: Graphic Organizers for Writing About Reading** presents background information addressed to teachers about these open-ended graphic organizers. Unlike story maps, story charts ask students to reach conclusions and generalize, to reason and hypothesize, and to think inferentially. Put several of the suggested generic categories on your chalkboard and have students construct their own story charts on large pieces of construction paper. (This will give them more room to write.)

PAGE 46 **Creating a Story Chart** serves as a template for you and your students to get started with story chart work.

Conflict Holds a Story Together

Name: _____ **Date:** _____

Stories always have action. An event happens to begin the action in the story, then other events—both big and small—move the story along, leading up to the essential conflict. Finally, important events occur that resolve this *conflict* and the story ends. The plot of a story is the series of events, but it is the conflict that is most important.

But what does the word "conflict" mean? How do we know when a conflict has been resolved? Why does an author include a conflict in the first place?

A conflict is like a struggle or a fight, though it can take a variety of forms. Conflict provides a center, or a purpose, for the characters' actions and for readers to be interested in those actions. Think about a long description of a pretty day in which two people sit having lunch on a picnic blanket. Now think about the same scene but with a tornado whipping up in the background.

Why does the second scenario sound more like a story? It's because a conflict, or problem, must be resolved.

The conflict usually occurs between the main character (the protagonist) and someone or something else. Even though there may be several conflicts in a book (such as all of the struggles that Harry Potter goes through), there is usually one main struggle that influences all of the events that occur. (In Harry's case, the main struggle is with another person.)

There are six basic kinds of conflict:

   ◆ person vs. person
   ◆ person vs. society
   ◆ person vs. beast
   ◆ person vs. the elements/nature
   ◆ person vs. himself/herself
   ◆ person vs. destiny or the future

Authors of picture books, novels, and chapter books all focus their stories on one or another of these conflicts.

Directions: Quietly read through the picture books at this center with a small group of other students. Discuss your thoughts about the conflict in each of the books. To determine the conflict, ask these questions:

   • *What is the struggle in this book?*
   • *What is the main character's goal?*
   • *What is the main character trying to do?*

Use the list of six conflicts above to identify the kind of conflict at work in each of the ten books. Find the appropriate category on page 34, then write the books' titles and their authors in the corresponding boxes. (You may need more boxes for some categories and fewer for others; use the back of the sheet to add boxes.) Afterward, discuss with your group what you learned and what you felt was difficult to understand. If anyone disagrees about the category for a book's conflict, discuss the different opinions, providing reasons, and see if you can come to a consensus.

Independent Reading Activities That Keep Kids Learning... While You Teach Small Groups • Scholastic Professional Books

The main character against another character
(person vs. person)

Title:

Author:

Title:

Author:

The main character against several other characters
(person vs. society)

Title:

Author:

Title:

Author:

The main character against a beast or beast-like character
(person vs. beast)

Title:

Author:

Title:

Author:

The main character against the forces of nature
(person vs. the elements—earthquakes, hurricanes, tidal waves, etc.)

Title:

Author:

Title:

Author:

The main character in conflict with himself/herself
(person vs. himself/herself—the struggle may be to make a decision, to take a course of action, etc.)

Title:

Author:

Title:

Author:

The main character against fate
(person vs. destiny—the struggle may include trying to change something that is supposed to happen.)

Title:

Author:

Title:

Author:

Independent Reading Activities That Keep Kids Learning... While You Teach Small Groups • Scholastic Professional Books.

It Depends on Your Point of View

Name: _____ **Date:** _____

Who is telling the story you are reading? Is it one of the characters? If one of the characters is telling the story, you—the reader—can learn only what that one character knows. In other words, you are seeing this story through only one pair of eyes, that particular character's eyes. This is called a *personal* point of view. There are two kinds of personal points of view:

1. If the word "I" is used as the story is being told, then you know that it is a *first person* point of view.

2. If someone else is telling the story, and you learn only what that one character knows or sees and not what anyone else is thinking, that is a *third person* point of view. (It's funny, but there is no such thing as a second person point of view.)

On the other hand, some stories let you in on the thoughts of all the characters so that you know what each one is doing and thinking. Stories like this are told from what is called an *omniscient (all-knowing)* point of view. The storyteller, or narrator, knows and tells everything about everybody involved.

Directions: Read some of the picture books available at this center. Think, too, about any of the chapter books or novels you have read recently. Then fill in the chart below. After you have completed the chart, use another sheet of paper to describe what you discovered about the point of view of the books you enjoyed the most and those you enjoyed the least. Attach that sheet to this page.

BOOK TITLE	POINT OF VIEW
1.	
2.	
3.	
4.	
5.	
6.	
7.	
8.	

Independent Reading Activities That Keep Kids Learning… While You Teach Small Groups • Scholastic Professional Books

Show What You Know

Name: _____

Date: _____

Directions: Show what you know. List the title, genre, point of view, and type of conflict for ten of the picture books at this center.

Book Title	What is the genre?	What is the point of view?	What is the main conflict?
1.			
2.			
3.			
4.			
5.			
6.			
7.			
8.			
9.			
10.			

Independent Reading Activities That Keep Kids Learning . . . While You Teach Small Groups • Scholastic Professional Books

The Good Guys and the Bad Guys

Name: _____ **Date:** _____

The main characters in stories are often referred to in literary terms. The main character, who is usually the "good guy" or the hero or heroine of a story, is called a *protagonist*. Harry Potter is an example of a protagonist. The "bad guy," or a main character who may cause problems for the protagonist, is called the *antagonist*. Voldemort is just one of the many "bad guys" Harry Potter comes up against. Voldemort is definitely an antagonist.

Directions: For this center activity, your job is to:

✦ Read five different picture books and determine who the protagonist and antagonist are in each of them.

✦ On a separate sheet of paper, create one question you'd like to ask each protagonist and antagonist. Attach that sheet to this page.

Book Title:	
Protagonist:	Antagonist:

Book Title:	
Protagonist:	Antagonist:

Book Title:	
Protagonist:	Antagonist:

Book Title:	
Protagonist:	Antagonist:

Book Title:	
Protagonist:	Antagonist:

A *Choice Menu:* The Secret Knowledge of Grownups *by David Wisniewski*

Name: _____ **Date:** _____

Directions: Sssssshhhhhhhh! This book has secret information. You are about to learn the real reasons for some of those rules grown-ups make, and some odd facts, to boot! Read the introduction to find out how the information was discovered, then read the book with a partner. Together with your partner, choose three questions from each column (for a total of nine), and write your answer to each question in the box provided. Each of you must write your own answers and turn in your own paper, but you may discuss your ideas.

1. Are vegetables really good for you, or is there another reason why you should eat them?		**10.** Which vegetable was given its name after thousands of them plunged over a cliff?
	6. What brought the Age of Vegetables to a close?	
2. Is milk really good for you, or is the government involved in some way?		**11.** How many cows do all the work? Give their names and locations.
	7. Why is combing one's hair especially important for boys with short hair?	
3. What are nature's solutions for ingrown hair?		**12.** Is blowing bubbles in your milk really rude, or is there another reason why you should never do it?
	8. What is the single biggest reason you should never play with your food?	
4. Jumping on the bed might have serious consequences. What could happen?		**13.** What's the difference between a feral mattress and a domestic one?
	9. What is the most important reason for not biting your fingernails?	
5. Picking one's nose is gross and disgusting, but it's not the real reason why you should stop this terrible habit. What is the real reason?		**14.** How will humming and flashlights help nosepickers?

Independent Reading Activities That Keep Kids Learning… While You Teach Small Groups • Scholastic Professional Books

Theme Talk

Name: _____ **Date:** _____

Directions: Read one of the books at this center. Choose and check ten of the words below. Then on a separate sheet write ten sentences. Each sentence must use one of the words you've chosen and must be at least eight words in length. Your sentences should summarize the story <u>and</u> discuss the theme of the book: What is it really about? What point does the author want to make? *(Note: You may add or delete prefixes and suffixes to the words you choose to use in your sentences.)* Attach the sheet with your sentences to this page.

Title of Book: _____

❑ abundant	❑ essential	❑ regrettable
❑ acceptable	❑ eventually	❑ reliable
❑ accurate	❑ evidence	❑ remarkable
❑ amazement	❑ exaggerate	❑ resist
❑ anxious	❑ exceptional	❑ sensible
❑ appreciative	❑ extraordinary	❑ shrewd
❑ astonishing	❑ foremost	❑ significant
❑ attitude	❑ helpful	❑ successful
❑ biased	❑ intelligent	❑ suggest
❑ bizarre	❑ interpret	❑ surprise
❑ caring	❑ miscellaneous	❑ tedious
❑ categorized	❑ motive	❑ troublesome
❑ compassion	❑ necessary	❑ trust
❑ complicated	❑ notice	❑ uncommon
❑ comprehend	❑ obvious	❑ undecided
❑ conflict	❑ oppose	❑ unexpected
❑ consequence	❑ optimistic	❑ unfamiliar
❑ consistency	❑ original	❑ uninteresting
❑ different	❑ outcome	❑ universe
❑ disgraceful	❑ pessimistic	❑ unknown
❑ distinctive	❑ powerful	❑ unusual
❑ distressing	❑ precisely	❑ valid
❑ eager	❑ predict	❑ valuable
❑ encouraging	❑ purpose	❑ various
❑ enjoyable	❑ qualified	❑ vital
❑ enthusiastic	❑ questionable	❑ well-known
❑ entire	❑ reasonable	❑ worthwhile

Multiple Perspectives and Thought-Provoking Stories: Five Easy Centers

Many children today approach books with the same kind of expectation that they have when they approach the computer. They think a bit differently than we did at their age, perceive a bit differently, and don't mind being immersed in something they don't totally understand. A growing number of picture-book authors and illustrators are creating literature with complex plots and multiple perspectives intentionally designed to foster a sense of disequilibrium. These multi-layered stories and their equally rich illustrations demand that their readers *think*. Although the ambiguity that is introduced may inspire a sense of fun and an opportunity for literary adventure, it could also create some frustration without sufficient preparation.

Children do not automatically leap the gap between literal and inferential comprehension. When teachers model thinking during read-alouds and share metacognitive musings, it not only demonstrates the process, but emphasizes the fact that text is meant to be interpreted. Begin by reading aloud from picture books and novels that demand discussion and require the constructing of meaning. Louis Sacher's Newbery Award-winning book *Holes* and Sharon Creech's *Walk Two Moons* are excellent examples of intermediate chapter books that have parallel stories that require analysis and synthesis. *Tibet Through the Red Box* by Peter Sis and *Golem* by David Wisniewski are picture books only by appearance; they are, in reality, sophisticated, problem-based mystical stories that invite commentary and evaluation.

The four authors included on the following pages—David Macaulay, David Wiesner, Anthony Browne, and Chris Van Allsburg—have written picture books that are definitely not superficial. These author/illustrators share common qualities:

◆ They require the readers of their books to fill in missing information.

◆ They expect interpretation.

◆ They write and they illustrate to create puzzles—so that there isn't one right answer.

◆ The literary devices they use include telling more than one story at a time, telling a story within a story, or offering differing points of view.

One way to approach the study of these authors is to examine their work on a whole-class basis and/or to read aloud some of their books to the class prior to beginning individual and small-group center exploration. When you are ready to establish centers, "Five Easy Centers," on page 42, should give you a good start. These center ideas offer application tasks that require revisiting books, rethinking concepts, reasoning, and hypothesizing.

Two related center ideas are presented on subsequent pages. In the first, on page 43, specific thought-provoking picture books extend the exploration of the imaginative and unusual kinds of books introduced in "Five Easy Centers." Such books will challenge

Independent Reading Activities That Keep Kids Learning... While You Teach Small Groups • Scholastic Professional Books

and enrich students who seem always focused on getting the "right" answers; for others who have had trouble personally connecting with text, the stories can help create that bond. Note: As you prepare this center, be sure to choose books that are truly challenging and remarkable. The second center activity, on page 44, is an in-depth and collaborative examination of one of the books by David Macaulay.

David Macaulay

David Macaulay's sophisticated picture book, *Black and White*, is fascinating—an excellent choice for intermediate students. Through four separate but connected stories and an essentially open-ended ending, the question, "What is black and white and red all over?" takes on a whole new meaning. And children whose gifts are specifically spatial and/or kinesthetic love the discovery factor in this book, which absolutely requires that the reader interact with the text.

Another of Macaulay's books, *Why the Chicken Crossed the Road* is a simpler offering, but again with a focus on cause and effect and a riddle that influences events. *Rome-Antics* has gorgeous art and uses ingenious perspective (the pigeon's eye view) to tell yet another wordless story about a homing pigeon who takes the scenic route in Rome. Because its focus is the architecture and the geography of Rome, this book may be better suited for older students.

David Wiesner

David Wiesner's books, *Tuesday, June 29, 1999*, and *Sector 7*, invite interpretation. Each is a wordless, or almost wordless, picture book. Because the lack of text requires genuine interpretation and there is a supernatural feeling about each, these books are more appropriate for intermediate students who will see relationships between the parts and infer their own story lines. Each provides opportunities for exploration, critical thinking and inference.

Free Fall, a Caldecott Honor Book, features winning illustrations that morph and transform. The storytelling is always offbeat and inventive, the focus consistently visual. Wiesner's newest book, *The Three Pigs*, is definitely "outside the box," with the three pigs finally folding the wolf into a paper airplane and sending him out of their lives. Wiesner interjects unexpected scenes that provide much fodder for conversation as he amusingly tells a much-updated and tremendously skewed version of the original.

Anthony Browne

Anthony Browne's book, *Voices in the Park*, is multi-layered—told from four different perspectives. The characters, interestingly, are not people but gorillas, and the story is related through dialogue during an afternoon in the park. The characters may be gorillas but that doesn't change the fact that readers will recognize a bossy woman, a man who is depressed, a lonely boy, and a lovely, optimistic, young girl. The illustrations provide insight into each character's mood, and the type style is changed for each of the story's characters.

Browne has also written *The Tunnel*, in which the pictures within the pictures and references to fairy tales provide clues as to the story's direction. While this is not a wordless picture book, the fact that it is a neutral, third-person narrative means that readers must infer insights into the characters' thoughts or feelings. Students will be making their own meaning and using their imaginations to fill in needed information. Work with

Independent Reading Activities That Keep Kids Learning... While You Teach Small Groups • Scholastic Professional Books

this book is especially rewarding for students in fifth grade and above.

Chris Van Allsburg

Chris Van Allsburg's books, *The Mysteries of Harris Burdick*, *The Wretched Stone*, *Wreck of the Zephyr*, *Jumanji*, and *The Widow's Broom* are among the very best of this picture book genre. And they have stood the test of time.

They possess a multitude of cryptic characteristics and puzzling motifs that do not allow the reader to be aloof. Students will find themselves grappling with and discussing what they don't understand. Van Allsburg creates magical worlds with mystical inhabitants; as an author he clearly enjoys being a bit weird, puzzling, and otherworldly. His illustrations engage the imagination as they tell the story, piece by piece.

Five Easy Centers

Focus on Just One Author. *Post these directions:* Read one of the books at this center. Work with a partner and create one *main idea* question, two *detail* questions, three *inference* questions and four *vocabulary* questions.

Compare and Contrast Two Books by One of These Authors. *Post these directions:* Which events in each of the books are unbelievable? Which events are believable? Think of a way to show the differences between the two books and the events that take place in each.

Compare Two Books by Different Authors. *Post these directions:* Focus on the illustrations. How are they similar? How are they different? How does perspective play a part? How does color influence the story being told? How much of the story is told by the illustrations and how much by text?

Cause and Effect Is a Predominant Motif in Most of These Books. *Post these directions:* What is the first event in the book? What happens as a result? For one of these books, chart the entire series of events and the action(s) that result(s).

What Makes These Picture Books Different? *Post these directions:* What are the specific characteristics of these picture books that make them look and feel different? Find three other picture books in the classroom or school library and compare them in detail with three books from this center. Focus on the story line and the characters. List as many ways as you can in which the center books are unusual.

Independent Reading Activities That Keep Kids Learning... While You Teach Small Groups • Scholastic Professional Books

Thought-Provoking Picture Books

Name: _____ **Date:** _____

Directions: The authors and illustrators whose books are at this center have something in common: they don't write or illustrate *ordinary* picture books. These books are worth reading, and the pictures in them are worth a closer look—they'll really make you think. If something is puzzling or strange in these books, it's been done on purpose. Think about that! Read several of the books and then decide which ones match the commentaries on the right. Write the titles in the appropriate place. More than one book may be listed.

Book Title	Commentary
	The illustrations are cleverly used to call attention to what is happening in the story.
	Whoever put this book together had a very vivid imagination.
	Both the art and the story create the feeling that something mysterious is going on.
	One event obviously causes another—much of the story unfolds as "cause and effect."
	The story is being told from an unusual perspective or from different viewpoints.
	I liked this book because I could use *my* imagination.
	Reading this book was like being inside a dream—a confusing one.
	I was still wondering and thinking about this book even after I finished reading it.
	Figuring out the plot of this story was like putting a puzzle together.
	There is definitely something unusual about the characters in this book.

Independent Reading Activities That Keep Kids Learning... While You Teach Small Groups • Scholastic Professional Books

Exploration With a Partner:
Black and White *by David Macaulay*

Name: _____ **Date:** _____

Directions: This is an interesting book to explore with a partner. You may work together and collaborate on your answers, if you wish, but you must each turn in your own paper. Be sure to answer Questions 1, 5, 6, 7, and 8 in complete sentences. Use a separate sheet of paper for your answers to those questions and attach it to this page.

1. David Macaulay doesn't write ordinary books. He likes to make his books different and interesting. After reading this book, what did you notice that was different and/or interesting?

_____

2. Circle the words and phrases that you think describe this book:

baffling   nebulous   an enigma   a puzzle

a conundrum   engrossing   inscrutable   ingenious

3. Which one of the words best describes this book? _____

4. How many stories were told? _____

5. Think of a title for each individual story. Write your titles on your answer sheet. Could all the stories be one story? Why or why not? _____

_____

6. Summarize one of the stories in one paragraph with four or more sentences._____

_____

_____

_____

7. What (or who) could the word "ubiquitous" refer to in this book? Tell why._____

_____

_____

8. Who, in this classroom, do you think would enjoy this book? Why?_____

_____

_____

Independent Reading Activities That Keep Kids Learning… While You Teach Small Groups • Scholastic Professional Books

Story Charts: Graphic Organizers for Writing About Reading

Story charts are really multi-purpose graphic organizers. They build comprehension by helping students organize their thoughts about what they've read. Story charts put thoughts into categories, and because they so neatly compartmentalize ideas and provide a structure for reflection, they appeal to students. When used as a prewriting activity after reading, story charts help students understand story elements and build paragraph sense.

To create your own story charts, simply insert your own categories into the basic template (see page 46). The essence of a story chart is its flexibility. That means you can create categories for anything you want reviewed, highlighted, or studied. Category selection is totally subjective and may depend on the complexity of the story as much as it does on the age and maturity of the children you teach.

There is also an open-ended quality to story charts because they can be used with novels as well as with picture books. With some adaptations, story charts can be used with nonfiction as well. A further benefit of this activity is that it works well with both heterogeneous and homogenous pairings/groupings. Students of varied abilities may brainstorm their story charts together.

It is important, however, that each student independently complete his or her own chart. An organizer like this is really the means to an end; each student can use the story chart categories as the topics of paragraphs. The paragraphs then become the substance of a report or essay.

Because the story chart serves as an organizer and is not a finished product, it is important that students use abbreviated phrases rather than complete sentences. Encourage them to assume a note-taking perspective and to view the story chart as an informal device on the way to a formal draft.

Possible generic categories for story charts include:

◆ How were the characters influenced by where they lived or visited?

◆ What kinds of obstacles did the characters need to overcome?

◆ In which ways did the main characters act intelligently?

◆ In which ways did the main characters not act intelligently?

◆ How did the illustrations enrich the story?

◆ If you were in this story, who would you be and what would you do?

◆ What vocabulary intrigued you?

◆ What literary devices did you notice the author using?

◆ In what ways did the author keep your interest?

◆ Why was the ending satisfactory?

◆ Why would you read other books by this author?

To create story charts for specific books, simply fill in the names of the characters or refer to specific events in the books.

Independent Reading Activities That Keep Kids Learning... While You Teach Small Groups • Scholastic Professional Books

Creating a Story Chart

Name: _____ **Date:** _____

Directions: To answer each question, write brief notes to yourself in each of the boxes. Use that information to build paragraphs for each of the questions. Answers that are related can be combined to make one paragraph. (Example: One paragraph could incorporate both the antagonist's and the protagonist's goals.)

Who is the protagonist in this story? Who is the antagonist?	What is the protagonist's problem? What is the antagonist's problem?	
	PROTAGONIST	ANTAGONIST

What is the protagonist's goal? What is the antagonist's goal?		What does the protagonist do to reach that goal?
PROTAGONIST	ANTAGONIST	

What does the antagonist do to reach that goal?	What happens after that?	What did you like about the way this story was told?
	What did the author want you to be thinking about when the story ended?	

Independent Reading Activities That Keep Kids Learning... While You Teach Small Groups • Scholastic Professional Books

CHAPTER 4

Exploring Literary Genre

Historical Fiction, Mystery, Animal Stories, Folk Tales, and Sports

As you introduce children to a literary genre, you are helping them to develop a schema for that genre. With increasing experience reading in that genre, they form an understanding of its components and establish a cognitive base of expectations. For example, when children approach historical fiction, they know they will need to pay particular attention to the details of the time period, while in a folk tale, they should watch out for magical powers and themes about good and evil. This kind of literacy knowledge provides, in turn, a context for further literature experiences and gives students a richer base for all reading.

This chapter presents background and activities for several of the most popular and familiar genres: historical fiction, mystery, animal stories, folk tales and sports. Chapter Five covers two other major genres—biography and nonfiction. Together these two chapters provide students with a solid sampling of the many different genres that exist.

Historical Fiction

This genre allows readers to step into a world of information and details not available in textbooks. It nurtures an appreciation for memorable characters and provides an experience of history with a strong emotional angle. By looking into the past in this way, students gain a deeper understanding of historical events. Exploring this genre encourages students to be better critical readers in all the content areas and across all genres.

PAGE 51 **Bringing the Past to Life:** *Riding Freedom* by Pam Muñoz Ryan is a literature study appropriate for fourth-grade level and above. This activity provides an explanation of the genre for students and then offers options for choices in their response to reading.

PAGE 52 **Historical Fiction: Listening to Voices from the Past, Part 1—A Bibliography** is a multi-leveled bibliography of books from this genre. This page invites students to choose a book from the bibliography (or any other from this genre) and to read it in preparation for the subsequent activity.

PAGE 53 **Historical Fiction: Listening to Voices from the Past, Part 2—Reading Activity,** a choice menu, asks students to select any five of nine questions. Small groups are a good setting for this activity, especially since this will offer you a chance to meet periodically with students to discuss their books and to provide guidance so they can answer the questions more effectively.

PAGE 54 **Hooked on Historical Fiction: Kathleen Karr** calls upon students to read two of this author's books from an annotated list that is provided. Students are then instructed to complete the activity that follows based on these books.

PAGE 55 **Historical Fiction: Compare a Pair** is a generic choice menu that students can use with the Kathleen Karr assignment or with any two books of historical fiction.

Mysteries

In this popular genre, students explore these common motifs:

➤➤ Mysteries have strong and sometimes exaggerated characters.

➤➤ Mysteries usually begin because of the occurrence of just one simple event.

➤➤ Mysteries usually have "good guys" and "bad guys."

➤➤ Mysteries require protagonists to use their powers of observation.

➤➤ Mysteries, especially detective stories, require protagonists to test their theories.

PAGE 56 **Mystery Bibliographies 1 and 2** provides a one-page divided bibliography that separates titles into two lists so that students of differing abilities will be able to study this genre.

PAGE 57 **Sleuthing, Deducing, and Investigating** poses questions based on students' reading of one of the mystery books listed in the preceding bibliographies. The questions have been adjusted for difficulty and can thus help you accommodate students of varied reading levels.

PAGE 58 **Mystery Words** is a challenging vocabulary activity that doubles as a change-of-pace book report.

Animal Stories

This genre has two major sub-categories—stories about real animals who act as they are supposed to and stories about animals that talk and act like humans. Some of the fantasy animals read books, wear clothes, and sit down at a table to eat. However, even these animals display genuine animal-like behavior—for instance, wolves still want to eat pigs and owls still hunger for mice.

PAGE 59 **Animal Stories: A Bunch of Classics—Old and New** names a variety of animal stories, categorized as realistic or fantasy, and grouped by level of reading difficulty. Students are asked to read one book from either category, which they will then use as the basis for completing the activity that follows.

PAGE 60 **Animal Stories: Real and Make-Believe,** a choice menu, differentiates between the two types of animal stories. Children in small groups can read the same book, or even different titles, and work through the questions together.

PAGE 61 **A Literature Study:** *Dominic* is based on William Steig's wonderful fantasy animal story. It is appropriate for fluent readers at the fourth-grade level and above.

Literature studies like this one are an excellent way to challenge a small group of fluent readers to think more deeply about what they read, while at the same time allowing you to continue to "guide" their reading. A text set of six to eight books is needed—one book for each child in a small group. While you are still teaching skills and strategies, you are also offering tasks that nurture self-directed learning and independent thinking. Questions are both literal and inferential.

Although a literature study is teacher-led, students are able to maintain their self-direction because groups meet with the teacher only two or three times a week. The groups will meet without the teacher to discuss the assigned questions and to prepare their written answers for the guided lesson.

Folk Tales

This next section includes both classic and retold folk tales, and features tales representing many different countries and cultures.

PAGE 63 *Rumpelstiltzkin* **Is a Folk Tale,** the first student activity for this genre, includes both a definitional discussion as well as a list of titles. Students are asked to read ten of the picture books listed (or any ten folk tales) in preparation for a matrix they will later complete.

PAGE 64 **Folk Tales: Ten to Talk About** is a matrix that might eventually be used as a graphic organizer. Once students fill out the matrix and use the categories to summarize what they have discovered, the categories become paragraph topics for further writing. To bring in an oral language component, use the categories as a framework for an oral report on the genre. A small group of children could even conduct a panel discussion.

PAGE 65 **A Genre Study: What Kind of Books Do You Like?** is open-ended and designed for struggling readers or those just moving into chapter books. The reading level for the books named hovers around 3.0. Five different genres (animal fiction, realistic fiction, historical fiction, humorous fiction, and mystery) are explored. Note that while realistic fiction and humorous fiction have not been explicitly covered in the chapter, these genres should be quite familiar to students. Only a quick review, or mini-lesson, should be necessary to prepare them. Also bear in mind that some children may need to be taught how to create a "pyramid poem," which is an eight-line poem with one word in the first line and with each subsequent line having one more word than the previous line.

PAGE 66 **A Genre Study: Exploring Characters, Setting, and Plot** ties in to the preceding activity and reinforces genre vocabulary.

Sports

Sports is the topic of the next genre section, which comprises two separate activities.

PAGE 67 **Baseball, Football, Soccer, and More: Books About Sports** by Dan Gutman provides options for choice in reading, but all the books are about sports. Students will answer three questions about each of the books they read.

PAGE 68 **A Literature Study:** *Honus & Me* is based on one of the books from the choice list on the previous page. Written at the fourth-grade reading level, *Honus & Me* is a delightful read, even if you don't particularly like baseball. Dan Gutman's blending of sports and fantasy is incredibly appealing. It is also very accessible for strong third-grade readers and up.

Bringing the Past to Life:
Riding Freedom *by Pam Muñoz Ryan*

Name: _____ **Date:** _____

When you read historical fiction, you are reading realistic stories that take place in the past but that have some element of fiction. In some historical fiction, the setting and the events are real, but the characters and the story are invented. Alternately, historical fiction can be written about people who really lived at the time, but the conversations and events are fictional, created by the author. The biggest challenge for an author of historical fiction is to make the story seem true. The fictional elements must be based on real research about the time period and the people. One of the best things about historical fiction is that it lets us travel back in time and find out through a story what life was like "back then."

Directions: Read this engaging book by Pam Muñoz Ryan. When you have finished, choose five questions to answer. You may discuss your thoughts with someone else who is reading this book, but your answers should be your own. Write your answers on a separate sheet of lined paper and attach the sheet to this page. Number all answers to correspond with the questions.

1. In what ways can you connect yourself to Charlotte Parkhurst? Use character trait words and personal stories.

2. Give some examples from the book that describe this particular time in history. What are some of the ways life was different then than it is today?

3. Compassion, cruelty, hope, and despair are behaviors and emotions that are simply part of life and so they are also a part of history. Find and describe scenes from this book that are instances of each of those behaviors or emotions.

4. How did Pam Muñoz Ryan get you interested in the main character?

5. Collect factual data from the book. Which of the data can you prove is true? How can you prove it?

6. Often the main characters in stories must overcome almost insurmountable odds. What were some of Charlotte's?

7. In what ways would you say that Charlotte lived out the dreams of her childhood?

8. What do you think Pam Muñoz Ryan wanted you to be thinking about when you finished reading this book?

Independent Reading Activities That Keep Kids Learning... While You Teach Small Groups • Scholastic Professional Books

Historical Fiction: Listening to Voices from the Past, Part 1—Bibliography

Directions: Reading historical fiction is a great way to be introduced to people, places, and events that took place in the past. Read one of the highly rated books below (or another book of historical fiction). Then follow the directions for the "Voices from the Past, Part 2" activity on page 53.

Title	Author
Adaline Falling Star	Mary Pope Osborne
Bluestem	Francis Arrington
Esperanza Rising	Pam Muñoz Ryan
Freedom Ride	Doreen Rappaport
The Fighting Ground	Avi
Sees Behind Trees	Michael Dorris
Ballad of Lucy Whipple	Karen Cushman
Jason's Gold	Will Hobbs
The Slave Dancer	Paula Fox
Bull Run	Paul Fleischman
In the Year of the Boar and Jackie Robinson	Bette Bao Lord
Lily's Crossing	Patricia Reilly Giff
Heads or Tails: Stories from the Sixth Grade	Jack Gantos
Tough Choices: A Story of the Vietnam War	Nancy Antle
Park's Quest	Katherine Paterson
The Purple Heart	Marc Talbert
The Story of Ruby Bridges	Robert Coles
The Watsons Go to Birmingham—1963	Christopher Paul Curtis
Grandaddy's Gift	Margaree King Mitchell
The Baby Grand, the Moon in July, and Me	Joyce Barnes
The Wreck of the Ethie	Hilary Hyland
Forty Acres and Maybe a Mule	Harriette Gillem Robinet
Sacajawea	Joseph Bruchac
Sybil Ludington's Midnight Ride	Marsha Amstel
Voices of the Alamo	Sherry Garland
This Generation of Americans: A Story of the Civil Rights Movement	Frederick L. McKissack, Jr.
Matilda Bone:	Karen Cushman

Independent Reading Activities That Keep Kids Learning... While You Teach Small Groups • Scholastic Professional Books

Historical Fiction: Listening to Voices from the Past, Part 2—Reading Activity

Name: _____ **Date:** _____

Book Title: _____

Author: _____

Directions: Select any five of the questions that follow and answer them on another sheet of paper. Attach that sheet to this page. Be sure to use complete sentences.

1. Is this . . .

    ✦ a fictional story about a real person?

    ✦ a story about something that really happened, but with fictional characters?

    ✦ a fictional story with fictional characters during a specific time in history?

2. In historical fiction, events are often viewed from the main character's perspective. In other words, the story is told with the main character as the narrator. Was this true of your book? If so, what kinds of dilemmas and controversies did the main character describe? If not, from whose perspective was the story told?

3. In what ways can you connect yourself to this book's main character(s)? Use character trait words, like "shy" or "talkative," and include personal stories.

4. Describe this period in history. How did the book help you understand this era? What factual information did you come across? What information did the book provide that can be supported with evidence from encyclopedias or other reference books?

5. What questions came to mind as you read? What questions do you have about the story, the character(s), or the time period?

6. How did the author get you interested in the story? Was it the characters, the story itself, or the time period? What made you keep reading?

7. Often the main characters in stories face almost insurmountable challenges. What were the challenges faced by the protagonist in this book?

8. What do you think the author wanted you to be thinking about when you finished reading this book? Share your thoughts in paragraph form.

9. On a scale of 1 to 10, with 10 being "absolutely excellent," how would you rate this book? Write three or four sentences that explain your rating.

Independent Reading Activities That Keep Kids Learning... While You Teach Small Groups • Scholastic Professional Books

Hooked on Historical Fiction: Kathleen Karr

Name: _____ **Date:** _____

Directions: As an author, Kathleen Karr is hooked on historical fiction. She calls this genre "…a time machine into the past." Karr works hard to create unique and memorable characters, immersing herself in research in order to make the people, the times, and the places she writes about believable. When she wrote *The Boxer*, she even put on gloves and learned how to box. Read any two of Kathleen Karr's books (listed below) and complete the activity on page 55, "Historical Fiction: Compare a Pair."

The Boxer (New York City, 1885)	**The Cave** (The Great Depression, 1930s)	**Gideon & the Mummy Professor** (Mississippi River, 1855)	**Man of the Family** (Early 1900s, immigrant life)
It Happened in the White House (spans 200 years to present)	**The Great Turkey Walk** (1860, the Old West)	**In the Kaiser's Clutch** (WWI period)	**Go West, Young Women** (1846, the Old West: first in a series)
The Lighthouse Mermaid (1800s adventure)	**Skullduggery** (1840, high seas adventure)	**Oh, Those Harper Girls!** (spoof of the Old West)	**Spy in the Sky** (Civil War, 1860s)
Go West, Young Women (1846, the Old West: first in a series)	**Phoebe's Folly** (second in the series)	**Oregon, Sweet Oregon** (third in the series)	**Gold-Rush Phoebe** (fourth in the series)

Which two books did you read?

1. _____

2. _____

Independent Reading Activities That Keep Kids Learning… While You Teach Small Groups • Scholastic Professional Books

Historical Fiction: Compare a Pair

Name: _____ **Date:** _____

Directions: Read two books of historical fiction and complete any <u>five</u> of the activities from the choice menu. Circle the numbers of the activities you choose. Write your responses on a separate sheet of paper and number them to correspond with the numbers of the activities. Attach the sheet to this page. *(Note: This activity may be used with the Kathleen Karr book list on page 55, or with any other two historical fiction books.)*

Book Title 1: _____

Author: _____

Book Title 2: _____

Author: _____

1. Describe the main characters in the two books by writing a telephone poem about each of them.	**2.** Which of the books do you prefer? What is there about that book that held your attention?	**3.** In what ways can you connect the main characters in each of the books? How are they alike? How are they different? Use character trait words and examples.
4. During what time period did these stories take place? In what ways are these books "time machines into the past"? What did you discover about the time period?	**5.** What literary devices are used? Is there humor? Are there flashbacks? Does the author use cliffhangers or foreshadowing? Provide examples from each of the books.	**6.** Collect factual data from the books. Research and provide more information about some of these actual events.
7. Compare the problems, conflicts and challenges that each of the main characters encounters.	**8.** Although these stories take place in the past, what are some of the events that could happen even now? Describe them.	**9.** What do you feel the author(s) of these books wanted you to be thinking about when you finished them?

Independent Reading Activities That Keep Kids Learning... While You Teach Small Groups • Scholastic Professional Books

Mystery Bibliographies

These lists include some of the most engrossing mysteries available for children. The list on the left (#1) may be more appropriate for struggling readers—students reading at the grade-three level or below. The list on the right (#2) is for those students reading at the grade-three level and above.

Mystery Bibliography #1	Mystery Bibliography #2
Cam Jansen and the Chocolate Fudge Mystery by David Adler	*Freddy the Detective* by Walter Brooks
The Case of the Scaredy Cats by Crosby Bonsall	*Basil of Baker Street* by Paul Galdone
Flatfoot Fox and the Case of the Missing Whoooo by Eth Clifford	*Alvin's Secret Code* by Clifford B. Hicks
A Case for Jenny Archer by Ellen Conford	*The Case of the Absent Author* by E. W. Hildick
The Robbery at the Diamond Dog Diner by Eileen Christelow	*Bunnicula* by James and Deborah Howe
Aunt Eater's Mystery Vacation by Doug Cushman	*Double Trouble Squared* by Kathryn Lasky
The Mystery of the Monkey's Maze by Doug Cushman	*The Bomb in the Besseldorf Bus Depot* by Phyllis Naylor
The Fine-Feathered Mystery by Carolyn Keene	*The Case of the Baker Street Irregular* by Robert Newman
Gumshoe Goose by Mary D. Kwitz	*Search for the Shadowman* by Joan Lowery Nixon
The Spray-Paint Mystery by Angela Medearis	*Match Wits with Sherlock Holmes: The Adventure of the Dancing Men* by Murray Shaw
Danger in Tibet by Robert Quackenbush	*The Time Machine and Other Cases* by Seymour Simon
M & M and the Halloween Monster by Pat Ross	*Casebook of a Private (Cat's) Eye* by Mary Solz
Nate the Great and the Pillowcase by Marjorie Sharmat	*Riddle of the Wayward Books* by Brad Strickland and Thomas Fuller
Nate the Great and Me: The Case of the Fleeing Fang by Marjorie Sharmat	*Detectives in Togas* by Henry Winterfeld
Detective Dinosaur by James Skofield	*The Case of the Goblin Pearls* by Laurence Yep
The Mud Flat Mystery by James Stevens	

Independent Reading Activities That Keep Kids Learning... While You Teach Small Groups • Scholastic Professional Books

Sleuthing, Deducing, and Investigating

Directions: Read one of the books on the mystery bibliography list (p. 56). Choose any <u>three</u> of the following six questions to answer. Circle those numbers. Start to write your answers on the lines below and continue on a separate sheet of paper. Use complete sentences. Number your responses to correspond to the questions you choose. Attach the sheet to this page.

1. Mysteries usually have strong characters. Were there any strong characters in the book you read? Describe them.	**2.** The reason that a mystery exists is usually that one simple event has occurred. What was the event in the book you read?	**3.** Detectives in mysteries must use their powers of observation. What does this mean? How were powers of observation important in your book?
4. Mysteries almost always have "good guys" and "bad guys." Who were the "good guys" and "bad guys" in your book? Make a poster showing them.	**5.** Detectives usually need to "test" their theories in order to solve the mystery. What "tests" were conducted in your book? Describe them.	**6.** Do you know someone who might like the book you read? Write a two- or three-paragraph letter trying to convince that person to read the book.

_____

_____

_____

_____

_____

_____

_____

_____

_____

_____

Independent Reading Activities That Keep Kids Learning… While You Teach Small Groups • Scholastic Professional Books

Mystery Words

Name: _____ **Date:** _____

Directions: As you explore different genres, you'll discover that there are certain words that readers of that genre use when they are discussing a book. Below are some words readers of mysteries might use. Read one of the books listed in the bibliography on page 56 and circle at least eight of the words below that you'd like to use in a report about the book. As the first part of your report, write out the definition of each of the words you've chosen. Then, use the words in complete sentences to describe what happened in your mystery. Use a separate sheet of paper for your report and attach it to this page.

Book Title: _____

Author: _____

suspenseful	curious	hypothesized	alibi
disappearance	suspected	questioned	mysterious
solution	crime	missing	predictable
clue	observed	deduced	details
evidence	justice	concluded	red herring
puzzling	sleuth	suspects	witness

Independent Reading Activities That Keep Kids Learning... While You Teach Small Groups • Scholastic Professional Books

Animal Stories: A Bunch of Classics—Old and New

There are two kinds of animal stories: those that are about real animals who act just like they are supposed to and those that are about animals that talk and act like people. Realistic animal stories could actually happen, but fantasy animal stories could never happen.

Directions: Decide which type—realistic or fantasy—you would like to read in the list below. The realistic books are shaded in gray. Books for older readers are in the top three rows of balloons. Read one of the books in the list below and then follow the directions on the next page.

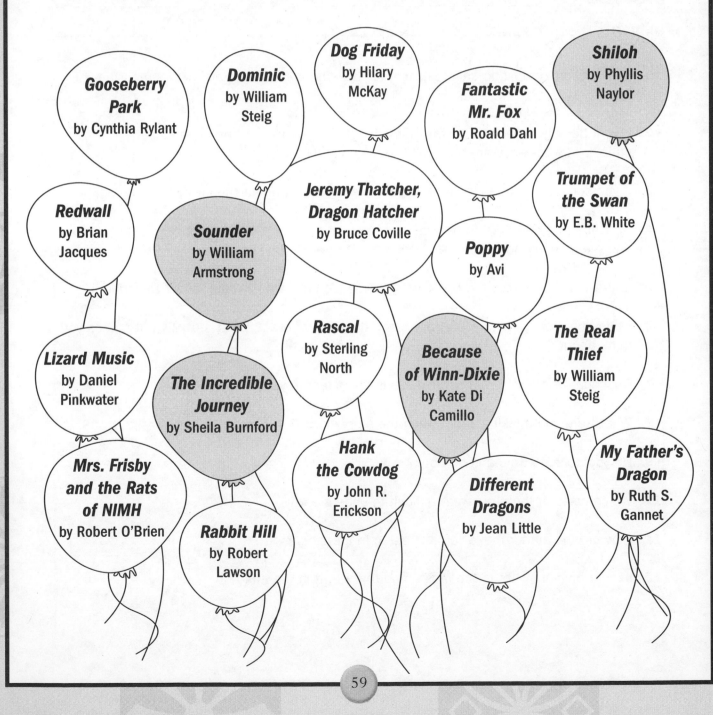

Gooseberry Park by Cynthia Rylant

Dominic by William Steig

Dog Friday by Hilary McKay

Fantastic Mr. Fox by Roald Dahl

Shiloh by Phyllis Naylor

Redwall by Brian Jacques

Sounder by William Armstrong

Jeremy Thatcher, Dragon Hatcher by Bruce Coville

Trumpet of the Swan by E.B. White

Poppy by Avi

Lizard Music by Daniel Pinkwater

The Incredible Journey by Sheila Burnford

Rascal by Sterling North

Because of Winn-Dixie by Kate Di Camillo

The Real Thief by William Steig

Mrs. Frisby and the Rats of NIMH by Robert O'Brien

Rabbit Hill by Robert Lawson

Hank the Cowdog by John R. Erickson

Different Dragons by Jean Little

My Father's Dragon by Ruth S. Gannet

Independent Reading Activities That Keep Kids Learning... While You Teach Small Groups • Scholastic Professional Books

Animal Stories:
Real and Make-Believe

Name: _____ **Date:** _____

Directions: Choose four questions that you'd like to answer about the animal story you selected from the previous page. Answer each question in paragraph form on another sheet of paper. Use numbers that correspond to the numbers of the questions. Attach your answer sheet to this page.

Book Title: _____

Author: _____

1. If your book is realistic animal fiction, tell how the animal/animals is/are important to the story.

2. If your book is an animal fantasy, describe the ways in which the animals behave like people. In what ways are they still like real animals?

3. If you could, what questions would you ask the author about this story?

4. Describe one relationship between a person and an animal in your book. Do the person and the animal understand each other well? How do you know?

5. Is there a scene from the book that you can picture vividly in your mind? Describe it.

6. Does this story remind you of any other story you've read? What story? What makes you think about it?

7. Describe several of the most important characters in your book.

8. What were you thinking about when the story ended?

9. Do you consider this a good book? Why?

10. Which parts of the story were difficult to understand?

11. How did the author make you interested in the story?

12. In your opinion, what is the most important event in the story?

Independent Reading Activities That Keep Kids Learning…While You Teach Small Groups • Scholastic Professional Books

Literature Study: Dominic

by William Steig

Name: _____ Date: _____

Pre-Reading Directions: Before beginning this book . . .
• Make up three questions you have about the cover.
• Read the information on the back cover.
• Answer this question: What is a fork in the road?

Vocabulary Directions: William Steig has a wonderful vocabulary. As you read, note any words that you do not know. First, try to figure out each word using context clues. If you are still uncertain of the meaning, list that word on a sheet of paper. Then look up the word in the dictionary and write down its definition. Using a separate sheet of paper, make a list of at least 25 words and definitions in this way. Attach the sheet to this page.

Chapter Reading Directions: None of the chapters in this book has a title; instead each has Roman numerals. After you have read each chapter, think of a really good title for it. Write the title on the line under the Roman numeral. Answer the questions, including the final overall questions, on another sheet of paper. Be sure to write down the corresponding chapter's Roman numeral before each answer. Remember to use complete sentences for your answers. Attach your answer sheet to this page.

I. ◆ In what way was the fork in the road important in this chapter?

II. ◆ In what ways were the witch and the catfish right?

III. ◆ Describe the Doomsday Gang.
◆ What was Dominic's predicament and how did he get out of it?

IV. ◆ Why do you think the author introduced the yellow jacket into the story?

V. ◆ Tell three things about Bartholomew Badger.

VI. ◆ What was the most important thing about this chapter?

VII. ◆ Describe the battle from beginning to end.

Independent Reading Activities That Keep Kids Learning...While You Teach Small Groups • Scholastic Professional Books

VIII. ✦ In what ways was Elijah wise?

IX. ✦ How did Dominic's philosophy of life differ from Lemuel Wallaby's?

X. ✦ In the morning, Dominic was overcome with exultation. What is exultation and what did he do to show it? Dominic also experienced indignation and compassion. Use the dictionary to look up those words. Explain why Dominic was indignant and why he was compassionate.

XI. ✦ Why did the Doomsday Gang consider Dominic a "fearsome creature"?

XII. ✦ Look up the names of the goslings in the dictionary. What did you learn about them?
✦ Dominic felt marvelous after ridding himself of his encumbrance. What was his encumbrance?

XIII. ✦ What part did art play in this chapter?

XIV. ✦ Write a three- or four-sentence summary of this chapter.

XV. ✦ In what ways did olfactory information influence Dominic's day?

XVI. ✦ How was a magic word important?

XVII. ✦ We're almost at the end of the story. What happened in this chapter that reminded you of the book's beginning?

XVIII. ✦ What do you think about the predictions of the alligator-witch? Describe your feelings about the way Dominic was saved.

XVIX. ✦ In what ways did the ending surprise you?

Overall Comments: What is your overall opinion of *Dominic*? Would you recommend this book to a friend? Why or why not?

Independent Reading Activities That Keep Kids Learning…While You Teach Small Groups • Scholastic Professional Books

Rumpelstiltzkin *Is a Folk Tale*

....And so are *Beauty and the Beast*, *Snow White and the Seven Dwarfs*, and *Rapunzel*. Every country has its own folk tales, and many of those folk tales have become so familiar to us that we think of them as our own. *Beauty and the Beast*, however, originated in France, and the others named above came from Germany.

Folk tales began as stories that were told aloud and not written down. Parents told stories that they hoped would guide their children's behavior. Often they told stories to explain the beliefs of their culture or to understand nature. Folk tales are fun to read for many reasons, but mostly because there are themes that are easy to recognize. This is true even if the folk tales are from other countries because the themes are universal. For example, heroes and heroines earn rewards for mastering difficult challenges; good people win out over greedy ones; and poor and powerless characters outwit powerful ones. Wishes are granted, and witches, dragons, trolls, giants, humor, silliness, spells, and enchantment abound.

Directions: Use your knowledge of the Dewey Decimal System to locate the folk tale section in your library. (Folk tales that are picture books may be shelved in the picture book/fiction section by the last name of the author who created his or her own version of the folk tale. Folk tale collections will be housed in the non-fiction side of your library.) Read any ten of the picture-book folk tales listed below or any other ten folk tales that you discover on your own and then complete the activity on the next page (p. 64).

Billy Beg and His Bull: An Irish Tale by Ellin Greene	*Clay Boy: Adapted from a Russian Tale* by Mirra Ginsburg	*Coyote Steals the Blanket: A Ute Tale* by Janet Stevens	*I-Know-Not-What, I-Know-Not-Where: A Russian Tale* by Eric A. Kimmell
It Could Always Be Worse: A Yiddish Folk Tale by Margot Zemach	*King of Magic, Man of Glass: A German Folk Tale* by Judith Kinter	*Konte Chameleon Fine, Fine, Fine! A West African Folk Tale* by Christina Kessler	*Rhinos for Lunch and Elephants for Supper!: A Maasai Tale* by Tololwa M. Mollel
Rough-Face Girl by Rafe Martin	*Savitri: A Tale of Ancient India* by Aaron Shepard	*The Journey of Meng* by Doreen Rappaport	*The Dragon Prince: A Chinese Beauty and the Beast Tale* by Lawrence Yep
The Ballad of Mulan by Song Nan Zhang	*Bony-Legs* by Joanna Cole	*Baba Yaga and Vasalissa the Brave* by Marianna Mayer	*The Tale of Rabbit and Coyote* by Tony Johnston
The Maiden of Northland: A Hero Tale of Finland by Aaron Shepard	*The People Who Hugged the Trees: An Environmental Folk Tale* by Deborah Lee Rose	*Wishbones: A Folk Tale from China* by Barbara Ker Wilson	*Toad Is the Uncle of Heaven: A Vietnamese Folk Tale* by Jeanne M. Lee

Independent Reading Activities That Keep Kids Learning... While You Teach Small Groups • Scholastic Professional Books

Folk Tales: Ten to Talk About

Name: _____

Date: _____

Directions: List the titles of the ten folk tales or picture-book folk tales that you have read. Look at the categories at the top of the matrix. Put an "X" in the square if the sentence at the top describes something true about that folk tale.

FOLK TALE TITLE	A lesson is learned.	Wishes are granted.	A reward is earned.	There is humor.	There is cultural information.	Someone is outwitted.	A clever character gets into trouble.
1.							
2.							
3.							
4.							
5.							
6.							
7.							
8.							
9.							
10.							

Independent Reading Activities That Keep Kids Learning... While You Teach Small Groups • Scholastic Professional Books

A Genre Study: What Kind of Books Do You Like?

Name: _____

Date: _____

Directions: Read one book in each row. Circle the title of the book you've read. When you've read the genre you liked the most. On a separate sheet of paper, tell something you've learned about each of the genres. On another sheet of paper, create a pyramid poem about the main character for each book that you read. Attach all the sheets to this page.

Animal Fiction	*A Toad for Tuesday* by Russell E. Erickson	*Rats on the Roof* by James Marshall	*Third Grade Pet* by Judy Cox
Realistic Fiction	*The Boy Who Ate Dog Biscuits* By Clyde Robert Bulla	*The Bathwater Gang* By Jerry Spinelli	*Benny and the No-Good Teacher* By Cheryl Zach
Historical Fiction	*Next Spring an Oriole* by Gloria Whelan	*White Bird* by Clyde Robert Bulla	*Pioneer Cat* by William Hooks
Humorous Fiction	*Happy Burpday, Maggie McDougal* by Valiska Gregory	*Julian, Secret Agent* by Ann Cameron	*Tooter Pepperday* by Jerry Spinelli
Mystery	*Encyclopedia Brown Gets His Man* by Donald J. Sobol	*Nate the Great and the Sticky Case* by Marjorie Weinman Sharmat	*Cam Jansen and the Ghostly Mystery* by David A. Adler

Independent Reading Activities That Keep Kids Learning... While You Teach Small Groups • Scholastic Professional Books

A Genre Study: Exploring Characters, Setting, and Plot

Name: _____

Date: _____

Directions: Choose one book from the five different genres in the chart on page 65. Write its title in the first column. Name the most important characters, tell when and where each story takes place, and then briefly tell what the story is about.

TITLE	CHARACTERS (Who Is in It?)	SETTING (Where? When?)	PLOT (What Is It About?)

Independent Reading Activities That Keep Kids Learning... While You Teach Small Groups • Scholastic Professional Books

Baseball, Football, Soccer, and More: Books About Sports by Dan Gutman

Name: _____ **Date:** _____

Directions: For this author study, choose three books by Dan Gutman from the titles below. After you read each book, use a separate sheet of paper to answer the following three questions. Remember to answer all three questions for each book. Attach your sheets to this page.

1. What was the most interesting thing about the book?

2. What new information did you discover?

3. What do you think the author wanted you to learn from the book?

The Million Dollar Kick

Jackie Robinson by Herb Dunn*

Joe DiMaggio by Herb Dunn*

Babe & Me

Jackie & Me

Cal Ripken, Jr.: My Story

Johnny Hangtime

Honus & Me

The Million Dollar Shot

Baseball's Greatest Games

They Came from Centerfield

*Herb Dunn is the pen name that Dan Gutman used for these non-fiction books.

Independent Reading Activities That Keep Kids Learning... While You Teach Small Groups • Scholastic Professional Books

A Literature Study:
Honus & Me *by Dan Gutman*

Name: _____ **Date:** _____

Pre-Reading Directions: Before beginning this book…

Overall:
- Make up three questions about the cover.
- Read the information on the back cover.
- Go to the library and look up Honus Wagner in the encyclopedia. Write five sentences (in your own words) about what you discovered.

Dedication:
- To whom did Dan Gutman dedicate this book? What does the dedication say?

Introduction:
- Dan Gutman uses the Introduction to tell you about the main character before you begin to read the story. What does he want you to know about Joe Stoshak?

Chapter Reading Directions: Answer the following questions about each chapter. Use complete sentences. Write your answers on another sheet of paper and staple that paper to this page.

Chapter 1:
"Playing Hardball"

✦ What else have you learned about Joe Stoshak from this first chapter?

Chapter 2:
"Throwing Money in the Garbage"

✦ What does "throwing money in the garbage" refer to in this story?

✦ What do you know about Amanda Young?

✦ What example of foreshadowing does the author use to end this chapter?

Chapter 3:
"A Piece of Cardboard"

✦ What baseball facts are revealed in this chapter? (Note: The drawing on page 16 is another baseball fact!)

Chapter 4:
"All My Problems Are Solved"

✦ What was so important about what Joe found?

✦ Why is that particular card so valuable?

It's "finder's keepers," right? What do you think?

Independent Reading Activities That Keep Kids Learning… While You Teach Small Groups • Scholastic Professional Books

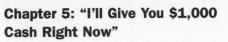

Chapter 5: "I'll Give You $1,000 Cash Right Now"

✦ What did you find out about Joe Stoshak in this chapter?

Chapter 6: "Floating on Air"

✦ Add five more factual sentences to your earlier research on Honus Wagner.

✦ Here's another chapter that ends with a bit of foreshadowing. What is it?

Chapter 7: "One Last Peek"

✦ Why did Joe finally decide that it really was Honus Wagner?

✦ What advice did Honus give Joe?

Chapter 8: "Daydreaming"

✦ What kind of time travel did Stosh and Honus plan?

Chapter 9: "The Argument"

✦ What was the argument about?

✦ What surprised Honus about baseball today?

Chapter 10: "Growing Up Fast"

✦ Why is this a good title for the chapter?

✦ What's a ducat, and who is Butts?

Chapter 11: "The Great Cobb"

✦ What does "The Antelope Versus the Buffalo" refer to? Why?

Chapter 12: "The Designated Hitter"

✦ Why does the title of this chapter have so much meaning?

Chapter 13: "The Other Half"

✦ There's lots of excitement in this chapter. What did you like best about it?

Chapter 14: "'Pros and Cons"

✦ What advice did Mrs. Kelly give Joe?

Chapter 15: "Going…Going…Gone"

✦ Two things were "going, going, gone" in this chapter. What are they?

Chapter 16: "On My Own"

✦ What question would you ask about this chapter?

Chapter 17: "Hmmmm, I Wonder"

✦ More foreshadowing. What makes you feel that this story doesn't quite end?

To the Reader:
What else does the author want you to know?

Honus Wagner's Baseball Tips for Kids:
What does Honus want kids to know?

Independent Reading Activities That Keep Kids Learning… While You Teach Small Groups • Scholastic Professional Books

CHAPTER 5

Centers That Build Nonfiction and Content Reading Skills

The guided reading group is the ideal place to teach the strategic behaviors necessary for reading nonfiction and interpreting content area text. In the small-group setting, students are more likely to engage in reflective conversation, receive direct feedback, and benefit from guided practice. Literacy centers, however, are ideal for offering students repeated opportunities to process content, engage in critical reading, and locate information independently. The activities in this chapter are designed to provide those kinds of experiences as well as to develop students' awareness of nonfiction genres. In these activities, students are asked to evaluate, analyze, compare, sort, and synthesize—skills unquestionably necessary for this information age.

Meeting Dewey: Moving Children into Nonfiction Reading describes eight great reasons why students need to know about the Dewey side of the library. Check it out!

 Dewey Investigations: the 500s and 600s sends children to the library shelves to investigate the topics found there, read a book, and create a cloze. (Page 28 provides a brief definition of the cloze technique.)

 Dewey Investigations: The 700s, 800s, and 900s is designed to encourage collaboration. Children work together to create questions and find answers to those questions.

 Stones, Bones, and Cyclones requires students to define their topics, then read three books in a row and write a six-sentence summary about each. Choices include paleontology, meteorology and archeology, among others.

 Phenomena: Nonfiction Books About Unusual and Extraordinary Topics is a two-page annotated bibliography of nonfiction picture books that focus on different phenomena. Students are asked to read the entire list, focusing on the phenomenon described in each entry. They will then choose one and read about it in preparation for a report.

PAGE 78 **Finding Fascinating Phenomena** provides a frame for the report mentioned above. The frame is an open-ended cloze activity intended to help students scaffold their expository writing skills.

PAGE 79 **Reading and Analyzing Biographies:** *Lives of the Athletes* and *Lives of Extraordinary Women* list the people featured in two different wonderful books of brief biographies by Kathleen Krull. Students read five biographies from each list in prepara-tion for questions they will answer in a subsequent activity.

 Biography Choice Menu provides the questions to be used with the Kathleen Krull books described on page 79, but the questions can also be useful generically for any biography.

PAGE 81 **Write in the Margins: Processing Content One Paragraph at a Time** teaches students to read content actively using a question-based strategy. This page includes a step-by-step guided lesson to help you introduce the strategy. Once you have taught it, provide nonfiction books and sticky-notes at centers for reinforcement.

PAGE 82 **Applying the Write-in-the-Margins Strategy (marked model):** *The Statue of Liberty* provides you with a sample text, marked as it would be after a student has successfully applied the strategy. You might also choose to use it as a guide for modeling the strategy with students during the introductory lesson.

PAGE 83 **Applying the Write-in-the-Margins Strategy:** *The Statue of Liberty* is an unmarked, reproducible version of the text excerpt for use in your classroom.

PAGE 84 **A Focus on Five** asks students to evaluate and rank nonfiction picture books and answer different questions for each book they have ranked.

PAGE 85 **Before You Open the Book …** proposes that children generate questions before and after reading a nonfiction picture book. This activity also focuses on vocabulary that is either new to a reader or specific to the content.

PAGE 86 **A Focus on Content: Using Picture Books to Practice Nonfiction Reading at Literacy Centers** provides an annotated bibliography of nonfiction picture books that can be used as the source for the previous two activities as well as offering students other reading possibilities.

Meeting Dewey: Moving Children into Nonfiction Reading

Melvil Dewey was born in 1851. During his 80 years, he made our lives much easier, but he probably drove his mother crazy. As a small child, he devoted hours to arranging his family's pantry to make it more efficient. This penchant for organizing continued while he was a college student, during which time he managed to revolutionize library science. Dewey devised a decimal system for classifying and cataloging books that is still in use around the world. His classifications divide nonfiction into ten broad categories:

000–099	**General Works** (encyclopedias and similar works)
100–199	**Philosophy** (how people think and what they believe)
200–299	**Religion** (including mythology and religions of the world)
300–399	**Social Sciences** (folklore and legends, government, manners and customs, vocations)
400–499	**Language** (dictionaries, grammars)
500–599	**Pure Science** (mathematics, astronomy, chemistry, nature study)
600–699	**Technology** (applied sciences, aviation, building, engineering, homemaking)
700–799	**Arts** (photography, drawing, painting, music, sports)
800–899	**Literature** (plays, poetry)
900–999	**History** (ancient and modern, geography, travel)

Following are eight great reasons why our students need to learn about the "Dewey side" of the library:

1. Students simply need to read more nonfiction. More than half of the content students will encounter on most standardized tests is based on nonfiction text.
2. Nonfiction informs. Many of our students lack the prior knowledge that brings meaning to learning. We must purposefully fill in knowledge gaps.
3. Many of our students don't read because they haven't found anything they want to read. Nonfiction offers broader parameters for choice.
4. The library/media center needs to be seen as a resource. Students need meaningful activities that require using it in that way.
5. The research skills that are practiced in the library/media center are themselves valuable tools for critical thinkers and analytic readers.
6. Children need to become familiar with nonfiction genres as well as fiction genres.
7. Reading nonfiction independently provides practice for the kind of reading required of content material.
8. It's a great basis for center work and long-term never-ending projects.

Children certainly do not have to memorize the different Dewey Decimal System classification numbers, but knowing about the library's organization is key to their feeling comfortable actually *using* the library for reading and research. The following activities, pages 73–75, are designed to help your students become familiar with Dewey. Some are center ideas and others tend to be more long-term projects.

Independent Reading Activities That Keep Kids Learning... While You Teach Small Groups • Scholastic Professional Books

Dewey Investigations: The 500s and 600s

Name: _____ **Date:** _____

Directions: Check your library's shelves in the 500s for books about dinosaurs, endangered mammals, fish, insects, planets, plants, and weather. Choose any five books shelved in the 500s and write their titles and Dewey Decimal numbers on the lines below. On the sixth line, describe what you think are the <u>overall</u> topics or subjects of the books found in the 500s.

_____

_____

_____

_____

_____

_____

Directions: Check your library's shelves in the 600s for books about pets, cars, cooking, building a house, understanding computers, and gardening. Choose any five books shelved in the 600s and write their titles and Dewey Decimal numbers on the lines below. On the sixth line, describe what you think are the <u>overall</u> topics or subjects of books in the 600s.

_____

_____

_____

_____

_____

_____

Directions: Read one of the books above and create a cloze with an accompanying word bank on another sheet of paper. Use vocabulary from the book that is new to you.

Independent Reading Activities That Keep Kids Learning... While You Teach Small Groups • Scholastic Professional Books

Dewey Investigations: The 700s, 800s, and 900s

Name: _____

Date: _____

This activity has two parts. You may do each of the activities with one or two friends.

Part 1 Directions: Visit the library shelves where the 700s, 800s, and 900s are located. Choose one book for each of the Dewey Decimal numbers below. If there are numbers beyond the decimal point, add them. Next, fill in the final column of page 75, titled "Dewey Decimal #," with the complete number, and write the title and author of each book on the chart. For "topic," describe in one or two words what the book is about. You and your friends may work together, but each of you must complete your own set of these two pages.

970. _____	917. _____	741. _____
736. _____	808. _____	921. _____
811. _____	793. _____	743. _____

(continued)

Title	Author	Topic	Dewey Decimal #
1.			
2.			
3.			
4.			
5.			
6.			
7.			
8.			
9.			
10.			
11.			
12.			

Part 2 Directions: Choose one of these books to read with your friends. Together, come up with twenty questions about the book and write them on a separate sheet of paper. Write the answers on a second sheet of paper. Take turns quizzing each other so that you know all the answers to your questions. Next, trade your questions and your book with another group. Read their book and answer their questions while they read your book and answer your questions.

Independent Reading Activities That Keep Kids Learning...While You Teach Small Groups • Scholastic Professional Books

Stones, Bones, and Cyclones

Name: _____ Date: _____

Directions: The words below identify nonfiction topics. First, use the squares to write a definition for each word. Then choose a vertical, horizontal, or diagonal row. Your assignment is to read a book on each topic in this row (a total of three books). Locate the books in the library. As your read the books, follow the directions below the chart.

Biography:	**Paleontology:**	**Sociology:**
Archaeology:	**Biology:**	**Meteorology:**
Astronomy:	**Psychology:**	**Botany:**

Directions: Fill in the boxes below as you read each book. Then, summarize each book by writing a six-sentence paragraph. Each sentence of your summary should contain an interesting fact about the topic of the book. Attach your summaries to this page.

Topic:	
Title:	
Topic:	
Title:	
Topic:	
Title:	

Phenomena: Nonfiction Books About Unusual and Extraordinary Topics

Directions: If you are the curious type, these books may be "right up your alley." In other words, they will probably be books that you will like. These are true stories about interesting people, faraway places, unique animals, and noteworthy phenomena. A phenomenon (according to Webster's Dictionary) is "any fact, circumstance, or experience that is apparent to the senses and that can be scientifically described or appraised, such as an eclipse." A further definition reads, "any extremely unusual or extraordinary thing or occurrence." The word *phenomena* is the plural form of *phenomenon*. Read this entire list, paying attention to the "extraordinary" things. Choose one book to read and report on. (Directions for a frame for your report are on page 78.)

A Walk in the Prairie
by Rebecca L. Johnson
How fire, forms, and fauna contribute to the phenomenon of the prairie.

Arctic Alphabet: Exploring the North from A to Z
by Wayne Lynch
The alphabet is used to present Arctic phenomena. For example, did you know that "L is for Lousewort"?

Birds in the Bushes: A Story About Margaret Morse Nice
by Julie Dunlap
Margaret Morse Nice is an ornithologist who wants to help others appreciate natural phenomena—even in their own backyards.

Galápagos: Islands of Change
by Lynne and Christopher Myers
These volcanic islands support phenomenally diverse forms of flora and fauna.

Ice Story
by Elizabeth Cody Kimmel
The phenomenal story of Ernest Shackleton who was shipwrecked in the Antarctic but survived.

Juneteenth: Freedom Day
by Muriel Miller Branch
When was it and why was it important? Two years passed before slaves in Galveston, Texas, learned they'd been freed by the Emancipation Proclamation. This book details the phenomenal happenings of Juneteenth.

Lives of Extraordinary Women: Rulers, Rebels (and What the Neighbors Thought) by Kathleen Krull
Short biographies tell the phenomenal stories of interesting historical women.

Monarchs by Kathryn Lasky
The mysterious behaviors of the monarch butterfly and other improbable phenomena scientists have witnessed.

My Season with Penguins: An Antarctic Journal
by Sophie Webb
Imagine a summer in Antarctica (yes, it's cold even then!) spent studying the penguins' habits and phenomenal behaviors.

Osceola: Memories of a Sharecropper's Daughter
edited by Shane W. Evans
Osceola Mays, a ninety-year-old sharecropper's daughter, tells the phenomenal story of her life.

Out of Sight: Pictures of Hidden Worlds
by Seymour Simon
Computers help create phenomenal photo-micrographs of objects that are far too small to be seen otherwise.

Pioneer Plowmaker: A Story About John Deere
by David R. Collins
The grain that was planted in the tough prairie sod created the phenomenal "breadbasket" of the United States—thanks to John Deere and the steel plow he invented.

Rio Grande: From the Rocky Mountains to the Gulf of Mexico by Peter Lourie
Phenomenally beautiful and full of history, the river is seen through the eyes of Lourie, an environmentalist and photographer.

The Lamp, the Ice, and the Boat Called Fish
by Beth Krommes
A phenomenal, true adventure about an Inupiaq family who became trapped in the ice during a Canadian Arctic expedition.

The Most Beautiful Roof in the World: Exploring the Rainforest Canopy
by Kathryn Lasky
Researcher Meg Lowman demonstrates that science is phenomenal work as she climbs dizzyingly up into the rainforest canopy of Belize.

Finding Fascinating Phenomena

Name: _____ **Date:** _____

Directions: What extraordinary things did you discover in the book that you chose? What curious, incredible, amazing, strange, and uncommon information did you read about? After you have finished reading the book, report on it by filling in the frame below.

The book that I read is _____

by the author, _____. I chose

this book because _____

and I discovered some phenomenal information.

I learned that _____, and

what makes it phenomenal is that _____

_____.

Another phenomenal fact is that _____

_____.

Furthermore, the author says that _____

_____.

What I found particularly interesting is _____

_____.

There are several reasons for this. The main reason is _____

_____.

Another reason is _____

_____.

Finally, reading nonfiction about unusual topics is really _____.

(Use a thesaurus to find an appropriate word to fill in the last blank.)

Independent Reading Activities That Keep Kids Learning... While You Teach Small Groups • Scholastic Professional Books

Reading and Analyzing Biographies

Name: _____ **Date:** _____

Lives of the Athletes: Thrills, Spills (and What the Neighbors Thought) *by Kathleen Krull*

Directions: Look through this book of short biographies and choose five of these amazing athletes to read about. In the chart below, put a check by those names you have selected. Then, using the Biography Choice Menu on page 80, pick any three questions for each of the personalities you've read about. Write your answers on a separate sheet and attach it to this page.

☐ Arthur Ashe   ☐ Sonja Henie   ☐ Pete Maravich   ☐ Wilma Rudolph

☐ Roberto Clemente   ☐ Sir Edward Hillary   ☐ Jesse Owens   ☐ Babe Ruth

☐ Maureen Connolly   ☐ Flo Hyman   ☐ Pelé   ☐ Jim Thorpe

☐ Gertrude Ederle   ☐ Duke Kahanamoku   ☐ Maurice Richard   ☐ Johnny Weissmuller

☐ Red Grange   ☐ Bruce Lee   ☐ Jackie Robinson   ☐ Babe Didrikson Zaharias

Lives of Extraordinary Women: Rulers, Rebels (and What the Neighbors Thought) *by Kathleen Krull*

Directions: Look through this book of short biographies and choose five of these extraordinary women to read about. In the chart below, put a check by the names you've selected. Then, using the Biography Choice Menu on page 80, pick any three questions for each of the women you've read about. Write your answers on a separate sheet and attach it to this page.

☐ Cleopatra   ☐ Nzingha   ☐ Tz'u-Hsi   ☐ Indira Gandhi

☐ Eleanor of Aquitaine   ☐ Catherine the Great ☐ Gertrude Bell   ☐ Eva Perón

☐ Joan of Arc   ☐ Marie Antoinette   ☐ Jeannette Rankin   ☐ Wilma Mankiller

☐ Isabella I   ☐ Victoria   ☐ Eleanor Roosevelt   ☐ Aung San Suu Kyi

☐ Elizabeth I   ☐ Harriet Tubman   ☐ Golda Meir   ☐ Rigoberta Menchú

Independent Reading Activities That Keep Kids Learning... While You Teach Small Groups • Scholastic Professional Books

Biography Choice Menu

Directions: Use this Biography Choice Menu along with the book lists on page 79 and follow the directions on that page.

1. Would you describe this person as courageous? Use factual information from the book to back up your answer.	**2.** What important lessons could be learned from this person's life?	**3.** What would you say were the major differences between this person and the rest of us?	**4.** Would you consider this person a role model for the way you want to live your life? Why?	**5.** Do some research in your library to find additional information about this person. Write down several facts.
6. What was offbeat or unusual about this person? What surprised or amused you?	**7.** Perseverance is described as believing in one's goals and not giving up. In what ways did this person show perseverance?	**8.** Did this person influence history? In what way?	**9.** Was it the willingness to work hard or a natural talent that made the difference for this person? How do you know?	**10.** In your opinion, what mistakes or poor decisions did this person make? What would you have done differently?
11. Do you consider this person a hero/heroine or a celebrity? How do you explain the difference?	**12.** What were the secrets of success for this person?	**13.** In what ways were this person's skills in communicating effectively and persuading others important?	**14.** Use the information in the biography to create ten interview questions you could ask this person.	**15.** Name five character traits that best describe this person. Justify (explain your reasons for) each of your choices.

Independent Reading Activities That Keep Kids Learning... While You Teach Small Groups • Scholastic Professional Books

Write in the Margins: Processing Content One Paragraph at a Time

The usual practice in many intermediate classrooms is to assign a chapter in the science or social studies text and to have students answer the questions at the end of the chapter. Because many students have trouble understanding the material, the usual result is that a large number of them do poorly on the assignment. Part of the problem lies with the practice of assigning difficult reading (many science and social studies texts are written above grade level) and not providing adequate support.

The strategy that follows actively involves students in processing content information by requiring them to create their own questions. It is a variation of "shared reading," using the overhead instead of "big books." It is particularly appropriate for intermediate students. By focusing their attention on key pieces of information, students learn what is important in content reading and at the same time practice test-taking skills.

You can introduce the strategy, via the guided lesson described below, any time during the year. Once you have taught the strategy, students can practice it at centers. It is suited for use with any nonfiction reading material, including magazine and newspaper articles, encyclopedia excerpts, or textbook pages. Students may work in pairs or small groups.

Be aware that most questions generated during this strategy will be on the literal level. However, since the purpose of the strategy is to help students take in and learn specific information, this is fine.

Note: A sample lesson, with questions marked in the margins, is provided on the next page. Following that is an unmarked version of the same material for use as a reproducible.

Introductory Guided Lesson

Materials Needed:
Overhead projector; transparency of the text material; a photocopy for each student of that material

Directions:

1. Distribute a photocopy of the text material to each student. Inform students that their task in this strategy is to identify factual information and to turn the information into questions.

2. With your transparency on the overhead, model the first few paragraphs for your students, thinking aloud as you locate facts and turn them into questions. Underline each fact as you find it. Write your model questions in the margins of the transparency. Go slowly and make sure that all students understand what facts are. Point out that any question written in the margin should be answered directly in the text.

3. Have students write their own questions for the remainder of the material in the margins of their photocopied sheets. (When this strategy is used with materials that can't be written on, students may use small sticky-notes and attach them in the margin.)

4. Later, have students use their questions and the answers as a study guide.

Independent Reading Activities That Keep Kids Learning... While You Teach Small Groups • Scholastic Professional Books

Applying the Write-in-the-Margins Strategy (marked model)

The Statue of Liberty *

Why was the Statue of Liberty built?

The Statue of Liberty was built to be a symbol of friendship between two nations—the United States of America and France. The statue itself was a gift to America from the French.

What was Frederic Bartholdi's idea?

A French sculptor, Frederic Bartholdi, came to the United States to speak to Americans about the idea of a statue celebrating freedom and liberty. When his ship sailed into New York Harbor, he saw a tiny island and decided that was where the statue had to be located.

What did the statue wear? What did she hold?

Bartholdi drew a picture of how he wanted the statue to look. It was a woman. She wore a very unusual crown, had on a long robe, and her right hand held a torch up high. He showed his drawings to President Grant and to other important Americans and then returned to France.

How did Alexandre Eiffel build the statue?

He made a 36-foot-high model of the statue before he began working on the real one. He divided the 36-foot model into 300 parts and made each one much larger before he put them together. He was going to build the biggest statue in the world. His friend, Alexandre Eiffel, helped him by building a supporting frame. It took a long time to build. Bartholdi couldn't finish it in time for the centennial celebration but he sent part of it: the arm with the torch. Each finger on the hand was larger than a man.

How long did it take to finish the statue? Where does the statue stand?

It took almost twenty years after Bartholdi first designed the statue for him to finish it. It was shipped across the Atlantic Ocean to the United States in 1884 in 214 crates. It was put together when it arrived. In 1956, the island on which the statue stands was renamed Liberty Island.

Why was this landmark important? How does the poem describe the immigrants?

Although the Statue of Liberty was given to the United States of America as a gesture of friendship, it has since become a well-known symbol of our country. Ships bringing immigrants to America entered New York Harbor, and the huge statue was the first landmark these newcomers saw. Emma Lazarus wrote a beautiful poem called "The New Colossus" which is on a plaque on the statue's pedestal. Welcoming those immigrants, the poem ends with these words, "Send these, the homeless, tempest-tost, to me, I lift my lamp beside the golden door!"

*Adapted from *The Story of the Statue of Liberty* by Natalie Miller (Children's Press, 1965).

Independent Reading Activities That Keep Kids Learning… While You Teach Small Groups • Scholastic Professional Books

Applying the Write-in-the-Margins Strategy

Name: _____ **Date:** _____

The Statue of Liberty*

The Statue of Liberty was built to be a symbol of friendship between two nations—the United States of America and France. The statue itself was a gift to America from the French.

A French sculptor, Frederic Bartholdi, came to the United States to speak to Americans about the idea of a statue celebrating freedom and liberty. When his ship sailed into New York Harbor, he saw a tiny island and decided that was where the statue had to be located.

Bartholdi drew a picture of how he wanted the statue to look. It was a woman. She wore a very unusual crown, had on a long robe, and her right hand held a torch up high. He showed his drawings to President Grant and to other important Americans and then returned to France.

He made a 36-foot-high model of the statue before he began working on the real one. He divided the 36-foot model into 300 parts and made each one much larger before he put them together. He was going to build the biggest statue in the world. His friend, Alexandre Eiffel, helped him by building a supporting frame. It took a long time to build. Bartholdi couldn't finish it in time for the centennial celebration but he sent part of it: the arm with the torch. Each finger on the hand was larger than a man.

It took almost twenty years after Bartholdi first designed the statue for him to finish it. It was shipped across the Atlantic Ocean to the United States in 1884 in 214 crates. It was put together when it arrived. In 1956, the island on which the statue stands was renamed Liberty Island.

Although the Statue of Liberty was given to the United States of America as a gesture of friendship, it has since become a well-known symbol of our country. Ships bringing immigrants to America entered New York Harbor, and the huge statue was the first landmark these newcomers saw. Emma Lazarus wrote a beautiful poem called "The New Colossus" which is on a plaque on the statue's pedestal. Welcoming those immigrants, the poem ends with these words, "Send these, the homeless, tempest-tost, to me, I lift my lamp beside the golden door!"

*Adapted from *The Story of the Statue of Liberty* by Natalie Miller (Children's Press, 1965).

Independent Reading Activities That Keep Kids Learning... While You Teach Small Groups • Scholastic Professional Books

83

A Focus on Five

Name: _____ **Date:** _____

Directions: There are several nonfiction picture books at this center. Read five of them. List the titles and the authors of the five books that you have read and rate them on a scale of 1 to 5 according to how interesting and informative you found each. (Consider 5 the highest rating and 1 the lowest). Each of the five books should have a different rating, with only one book receiving a 5. There are also different questions for each of the books. Answer them on another sheet of paper and attach it to this page.

#5 Book title: _____

   Author: _____

#4 Book title: _____

   Author: _____

#3 Book title: _____

   Author: _____

#2 Book title: _____

   Author: _____

#1 Book title: _____

   Author: _____

Book #5: What information did you know about this topic before you read the book? How did the author keep you interested in the topic? How can you use what you learned?

Book #4: How did the author of this book feel about the topic? What major points was the author trying to get across? How did the author convey feeling as well as facts?

Book #3: What surprised you? What did you learn that was new? How did the content increase your understanding of this topic?

Book #2: Why did you rate this book so low? If it was boring, what could the author or illustrator have done differently? What would you have done? If the topic interested you, but the book did not, what could you do to get more information on this topic?

Book #1: Compare this book to the one you rated #5. What is the same? What is different? What are some major reasons that make this the one you liked the least?

Before You Open the Book...

Name: _____ **Date:** _____

Pre-reading Directions: Choose a nonfiction picture book at this center. Before you open it, think of three questions that you have about the cover and/or the title. Write your questions here:

1. _____

2. _____

3. _____

After-reading Directions: After you have read the book, come up with six questions about it that begin with the words below. Answer the questions on another sheet of paper.

1. Who_____

_____?

2. What_____

_____?

3. Where_____

_____?

4. When_____

_____?

5. Why_____

_____?

6. How_____

_____?

Vocabulary Building Directions: Look back through the book for words that are new to you and for vocabulary that is specifically about the book's topic. Write those words below and define them on a separate sheet of paper.

Independent Reading Activities That Keep Kids Learning... While You Teach Small Groups • Scholastic Professional Books

A Focus on Content:
Using Picture Books to Practice Nonfiction Reading at Literacy Centers

This well-rounded, annotated bibliography of nonfiction picture books can be used as the book source for both "A Focus on Five" (page 84) and "Before You Open the Book…" (page 85). As well, it offers many other reading possibilities for your students.

Ammon, Richard *Conestoga Wagons* The role Conestogas played in our history.

Arnold, Caroline *Easter Island: Giant Stone Statues Tell of a Rich and Tragic Past* These huge stone statues have historical as well as cultural stories to tell.

Arnosky, Jim *Watching Water Birds* Information on fresh and saltwater birds along with delightful paintings by the author.

Bruchac, Joseph *Crazy Horse's Vision* The Battle of the Little Bighorn and Crazy Horse, brave defender of his people.

Collier, Bryan *Uptown* Travel around Harlem with a young boy as a guide. Wonderful watercolors and collages.

Curtis, Patricia *Animals You Never Even Heard Of* Twelve unusual, endangered, and rare species.

Janulewicz, Mike *Yikes! Your Body, Up Close!* Creepy photographs taken using an electron microscope, and "guess the body part" text.

Jenkins, Steve *The Top of the World: Climbing Mount Everest* Amazing collages, Tips on how to scale a mountain, and facts about this highest peak.

Jimenez, Francisco *The Christmas Gift* With text in English and Spanish, the poverty of a farm-labor camp and the love of family.

King, Wilma *Children of the Emancipation* Photographs and prints showing African American children at the time of the Emancipation Proclamation.

Knight, M.B. and Melnicove, Mark *Africa Is Not a Country* Children introduce us to different countries within this continent.

Laufer, Peter *Made in Mexico* A small village in Mexico influences music around the world in a most unusual way.

Lourie, Peter *Mississippi River: A Journey Down the Father of Waters* Adventures down the Mississippi by canoe along with stories of the river's past.

Marx, Trish *One Boy from Kosovo* A twelve-year-old Kosovo refugee shares the story of his life.

McMillan, Bruce *Wild Flamingos* These animals eat with their heads upside-down and flourish drinking salt water. Lots more facts.

Peacock, Carol Antoinette *Mommy Far, Mommy Near: An Adoption Story* A Chinese child adopted and brought to America copes with having two mothers.

Polacco, Patricia *The Butterfly* A French family hides a Jewish girl from the Nazis. The author's note adds even more depth.

Pringle, Laurence *Elephant Woman: Cynthia Moss Explores the World of Elephants* Elephant family structure, social life and communication. Beautiful photographs.

Rappaport, Doreen *Freedom River* John Parker bought his own freedom and then helped others find theirs.

Sinnott, Susan *Charley Waters Goes to Gettysburg* Charley and his dad participate in the reenactment of the Battle of Gettysburg.

Tsuchiya, Yukio *Faithful Elephants* The heartbreaking story of why the animals of the Ueno Zoo in Tokyo had to be put to death.

Tweit, Susan *City Foxes* The adaptations and survival strategies of a family of red foxes born in a city cemetery.

Weatherford, Carol Boston *The Sound that Jazz Makes* This history of jazz is accompanied by oil paintings and beautiful descriptive language.

West, Delmo C. and Jean M. *Uncle Sam and Old Glory: Symbols of America* Covers fifteen traditional symbols of American identity.

Wick, Walter *A Drop of Water: A Book of Science and Wonder* Beautiful magnified photographs with easy scientific explanations and ideas for experiments.

Wilson, Janet *Imagine That!* "Progress" (decade by decade) in the twentieth century, from the perspective of a hundred-year-old woman. Filled with fascinating facts about technology, inventions, and entertainment.

Independent Reading Activities That Keep Kids Learning… While You Teach Small Groups • Scholastic Professional Books

CHAPTER 6

It's About Words

Look It Up: Dictionary and Vocabulary Strategies

Watch your students when they're doing dictionary work. I'm convinced that sometimes they're just not sure whether the letter *r* does, in fact, follow *q*. I've even heard my intermediate students quietly singing the alphabet song just to make sure. Frequent use of the dictionary, or "the big red answer book," as we fondly referred to it in my classroom, reinforces a host of skills in addition to alphabetizing.

Here are some easy ways to get students into the dictionary as often as possible:

➤ **Hold dictionary definition races.** When I'm reading aloud and encounter a word I think the children should know, I say, "I wonder what that word means." It's a signal. The race is on to find the word in their dictionaries. Students stand as soon as they've located it. Require that all of your students write the word and the meaning before you call on anyone to share the meaning with the rest of the class. For those students who finish quickly, add the small task of writing a sentence that uses the word. This allows time for all students to succeed in finding the word. Later, ask for volunteers to share their sentences.

This is an excellent activity for small groups because struggling readers will have more opportunity to be directly engaged. And it's an opportunity for everyone to discuss multiple meanings, syllabication, pronunciation, and a host of other good things to know.

▸▸ **Create reasons to have students open their dictionaries every day.** The effective use of the dictionary requires disciplined practice. To make the practice meaningful, tie it in with the literature you read aloud to your children. Once as I was reading *Poppy* (by Avi), I came upon the sentence "Lungwort dipped his head in acknowledgment of the tribute." I did not keep reading. "Hmmm," I said to the students, "What do you think he did?" They all knew he dipped his head. We dipped our heads. "But why?" I asked. "I guess we'd better look up some words." I wrote the sentence on the board and underlined "acknowledgment" and "tribute." What's the next best step? When reading aloud, it is good educational practice to simply stop and explain the word. After the reading, however, you can follow up with the activity below.

▸▸ **Use index cards to record new vocabulary words.** For each student, provide 25 to 30 index cards that will go inside a small zipper-topped plastic bag. The children write a new word on one side of the card and the definition on the other side.

▸▸ **Extend activities with those new words.** Ask students to put words into sentences that they then rewrite, using synonyms. They can also find antonyms for the new words (in classroom books, dictionaries, or by brainstorming), and quiz themselves and each other on meanings. Or you might have them play "Vocabulary Concentration," a game that evolved as I was trying to provide continuing reinforcement for new vocabulary words. The children simply take out their index cards, lay them on the floor or table with the definitions up and then take turns guessing the vocabulary word on the opposite side. The advantage to having the definition face-up is that children read and reread it, and the repetition helps the information "stick." With the vocabulary word on the other side of the card, there is only one word to remember.

▸▸ **Construct a crossword puzzle of recent words.** As they make their puzzles, students should use the definitions of the new words as the puzzle clues. A variation for clues is to have them write sentences with the new word omitted.

▸▸ **Create word sorts, finding categories into which the words will fit.** Children head back to the dictionary to figure out the categories (e.g., nouns, adjectives, verbs, and so on).

▸▸ **Create alliterative sentences.** The new words become the key words around which sentences will be built. Students head back to the dictionary to find words beginning with the same letter.

▸▸ **Define content words.** Once defined, content words need to be reinforced by activities that add meaning and aid memory. Try any of the above three ideas or a topic-focused, student-created alphabet book. One teacher with whom I've worked created a pocket dictionary for each new unit of study, and it actually fit into her students' pockets. They loved the novelty of it.

▶▶ **Make use of vocabulary webs.** Using an overhead transparency, place the title of the book or chapter in the center of the web. Target those words you suspect may cause comprehension difficulties and put them at the ends of the spokes. Provide each student with a photocopy of the web. Introduce the words prior to reading the book or chapter aloud, and stop and simply explain the word when you come to it, jotting down its meaning at the end of the spoke. When you have finished reading, ask students to add a spoke from each word and write in the dictionary definition. (See page 91 for a sample vocabulary web.)

▶▶ **Rewrite definitions to fit into sentences.** In this activity, students paraphrase dictionary definitions so that each definition fits and works within a given sentence.

▶▶ **Play "Vocabulary Tic-Tac-Toe."** Distribute to students cards with blank grids of nine squares (three across and three down). Then call out words (or put them on the chalkboard) and have students write them randomly into their grids (stress *randomly*, so students' words are in different places). Once the words are written down, give the definition of the word and have students "X" it out or cover it. When a student has covered three vertically, diagonally or horizontally, he or she calls out "Three in a Row." The student must be able to give the definitions of the three words. Continue playing until all the words are covered. Children usually find this game a lot of fun.

These activities and those that follow can be adapted for use in teacher-directed instruction or

for practice in literacy centers. Work can be done independently or in collaboration with other students. The following activities and teacher pages, summarized below, make up the remainder of this chapter.

PAGE 91 **Vocabulary Web for *The Great Turkey Walk*** by Kathleen Karr is a strategy for sharing words with children prior to reading. In this activity, it's applied to a wonderful, funny story, but it can be used with just about any book. I like the vocabulary web because it's not a list. It limits the number of words we introduce and allows us to focus on words that are really essential to the story. Choose words that students will not know as you read aloud or as they read to themselves. Incidentally, this book is about 15-year-old Simon, who has repeated third grade three times. His teacher "graduates" him and then helps him "find his wings." It's an appealing book about perseverance.

PAGE 92 **Vocabulary Web** is a template for creating your own webs. Use it yourself or put it at a center so that your students can write in the words that they need to look up. They are directed to add a spoke to each oval for each word's definition. (Students' during-reading use of the strategy is a variation of its more typical use.)

PAGE 93 **Words That Work: Great Adjectives for Character Descriptions** introduces character trait words for students to use when describing characters in their books. Students are asked to define the words they select and use them in sentences.

PAGE 94 **A Study of the Characters: *Because of Winn-Dixie*** asks students to choose three words that befit each character. Students then define each word and use it in a sentence that aptly describes the character. Next, students turn the three sentences into a paragraph, and ultimately use the paragraphs to build an essay or report. *Because of Winn-Dixie*, by Kate DeCamillo, is a 2001 Newbery Honor Medal winner; it is a beautifully written story with wonderfully memorable characters, making it the perfect subject for this activity.

PAGE 95 **Character Commentary** provides a generic way to use the above vocabulary-building activity with any book.

PAGE 96 **ABC: Adjectives Build Character** expands upon the preceding activity, taking it to the next level. For students reading more advanced material, these challenging activities represent greater complexity and open-endedness.

PAGE 98 **Making Sense of New Vocabulary:** *The Green Book* includes two activities; together they build students' background knowledge and awareness of context, thus helping to prepare them for reading. To start, vocabulary that may be difficult is introduced prior to reading. Students check words they do not know and look up their definitions. Afterward, they insert each word into its appropriate sentence and write the entire set of sentences. Whether read aloud or used with a small group, *The Green Book*, by Jill Paton Walsh, is a wonderful way to introduce children to science fiction as a genre. This activity has accountability built in.

PAGE 99 **Wordplay: It's Pun and Games** details the word collections you can start in your classroom. Building an appreciation for words isn't difficult if you add an element of fun. (For instance, did you know that one well-known children's book protagonist has a palindromic full name, with his last name a "semordnilap" of his first!)

PAGE 101 **Heteronyms: Playing With Words** is a dictionary-based activity, ideal for collaborative center work. Just in case you weren't sure—a heteronym is a word like "minute" that can be pronounced two different ways and have two different meanings.

PAGE 103 **Poetry for Different Purposes** details several poetry formats that have great utility in the classroom. Students can write poetry at centers to summarize a reading assignment, including a chapter in their science or social studies books, or to bring closure to a unit of study. They can write poems about the characters in a story, about plots, about literary elements, or to show what they have learned in any subject area. Poetry is, of course, all about words; writing it can help students learn about words in brand-new ways.

Vocabulary Web for
The Great Turkey Walk *by Kathleen Karr*

Directions: There are several words you may not know when your teacher reads this book aloud to you or when you read it to yourself. Look up each of the words below. Draw a spoke from each oval and write a brief definition at the end of the spoke. Now, when you hear or read these words, you'll know what they mean.

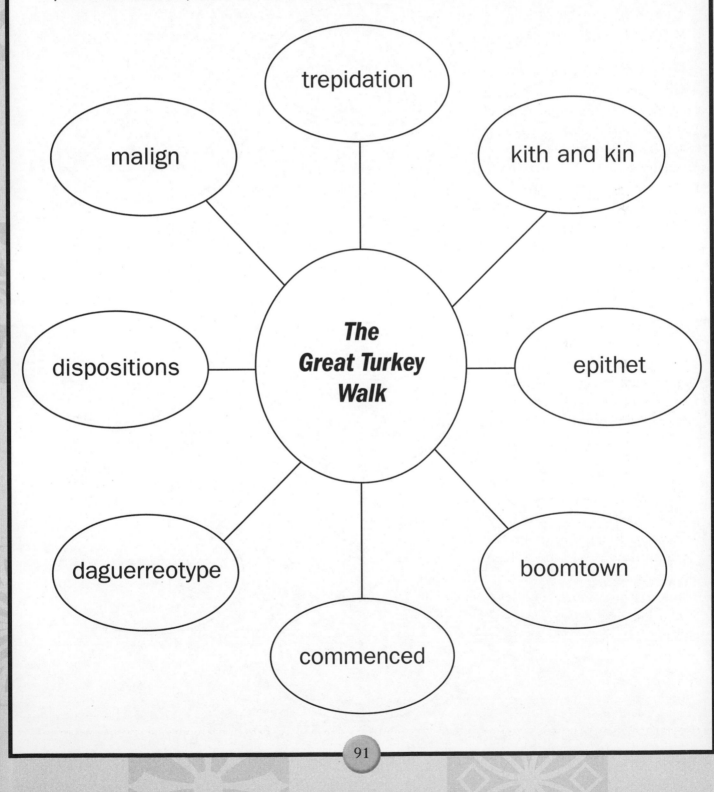

Independent Reading Activities That Keep Kids Learning... While You Teach Small Groups • Scholastic Professional Books

91

Vocabulary Web

Name: _____   **Date:** _____

Directions: Write the title of your book in the center of the web. As you read, write unfamiliar words in the ovals. Then look these words up in the dictionary. Draw a spoke from each oval and write a brief definition at the end of the spoke.

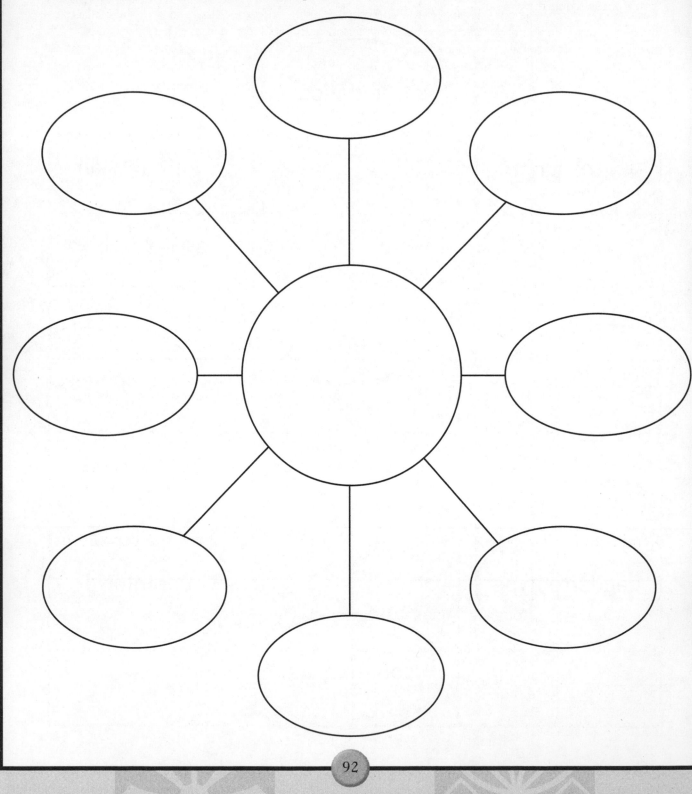

Independent Reading Activities That Keep Kids Learning... While You Teach Small Groups • Scholastic Professional Books

Words That Work: Great Adjectives for Character Descriptions

Name: _____ **Date:** _____

Directions: Read two books at this center. On a separate sheet of paper, make a list of the characters in each book. Then, circle one word from each column below to describe those characters. (Look words up in the dictionary if you don't know their meanings.) Write the appropriate words next to the characters' names and then write the definitions for the words. Finally, write one sentence for each word circled that tells something about the character or the story. (Example: Opal was *eager* to get Winn-Dixie out of the store.) Attach the separate sheet to this page.

adaptable	affable	ambitious	aggressive	analytical	bold
calm	capable	cautious	charming	cheerful	competent
considerate	daring	dignified	eager	forceful	fair-minded
intellectual	intrepid	mature	organized	original	outgoing
painstaking	patient	persevering	polite	proud	rational
reflective	relaxed	robust	sharp-witted	spunky	supportive
tactful	tough	unassuming	unexcitable	wholesome	wary
watchful	well-balanced	whimsical	wily	wordy	worthy

A Study of the Characters:
Because of Winn-Dixie *by Kate DiCamillo*

Name: _____ **Date:** _____

Directions: Think carefully about what makes each character in this book unique. Then look through the words in the "Words That Work: Great Adjectives for Character Descriptions" chart on page 93. Look up any words you don't know. Choose three words to describe each of the characters named below and write definitions for the words you chose. (Note that the last "character" is Opal's dog, Winn-Dixie.) On a separate sheet of paper, write a sentence for each word, using evidence from the story to show why that character trait fits that particular character.

Combine your sentences to make a short paragraph about each character. Each paragraph must have at least three sentences, one for each word. Conclude by writing a final paragraph about Winn-Dixie and his importance to this very special story. When you've completed this assignment, you should have a seven-paragraph report. Use extra paper if you need, and attach your sheets of paper to this page

Character	#1	#2	#3
Opal			
The Preacher			
Miss Franny Block			
Gloria Dump			
Amanda			
Otis			
Winn-Dixie			

Independent Reading Activities That Keep Kids Learning... While You Teach Small Groups • Scholastic Professional Books

Character Commentary

Name: _____ **Date:** _____

Directions: In the left-hand column, list the names of the most important characters of a favorite book. Decide on three words to describe each of those characters. Choose your words carefully. (You may use the adjectives from the "Words That Work" chart on page 93 or you may use other suitable adjectives.) On a separate sheet of paper, write a sentence for each word. Combine the three sentences into one paragraph about that character. The paragraph you write must describe the actions and importance of the character in the story. Then, combine the paragraphs into one report. The report should have the same number of paragraphs as there are characters. Finally, write a concluding paragraph that includes your opinion of the book, your personal commentary on the characters, and whether or not you'd recommend this book to a friend. Attach your report to this page.

Title: _____

Author: _____

Character's Name	Character Trait #1	Character Trait #2	Character Trait #3

Independent Reading Activities That Keep Kids Learning… While You Teach Small Groups • Scholastic Professional Books

ABC: Adjectives Build Character

Name: _____ **Date:** _____

Directions: This activity is a follow-up to "Character Commentary" on page 95. By completing that activity, you will have formed a clear idea about the characters in a favorite book. Now you have a chance to expand on your opinions and think about the same characters in different ways. Answer the following questions on the lines provided here and on page 97.

Book Title: _____

Author: _____

1. Of the characters you listed, which ones do you like? Explain why, using any of the adjectives in your "Character Commentary" chart.

_____

_____

_____

_____

_____

_____

_____

2. Do any of the characters remind you of yourself? Which ones? How are you alike? (Again, use any of the adjectives on the chart.)

_____

_____

_____

_____

_____

_____

_____

_____

3. Are there any characters you don't like? Who are they? What negative character traits do they have? (You may add prefixes to the adjectives in your "Character Commentary" chart.)

_____

_____

_____

_____

_____

_____

_____

4. How did you feel about the way the book ended? (Tell how the events in the book left you <u>feeling</u>, not whether you liked the book or not.)

_____

_____

_____

_____

_____

_____

_____

5. Which character(s) do you think influenced the resolution of the story? Whose actions were the <u>most</u> critical in resolving the conflict / problem? Describe those actions. Which character traits were most important in that character's final actions?

_____

_____

_____

_____

_____

_____

_____

Independent Reading Activities That Keep Kids Learning… While You Teach Small Groups • Scholastic Professional Books

Making Sense of New Vocabulary:
The Green Book *by Jill Paton Walsh*

Name: _____ Date: _____

Pre-Reading Directions: You may encounter some new vocabulary words in this book. Before reading *The Green Book*, check the words below whose meanings you do not already know. Look up those words and write down their definitions on a separate piece of paper. The vocabulary is important to understanding this book.

hexagonal	gadget	allocated	amphitheater
biorhythms	coincidence	contrive	dwindling
stores	crimson	hostile	aloft
straggling	solemn	precious	technology

After-Reading Directions: When you have finished reading the book, use the definitions to help you fill in the correct words below.

1. "There are signs of very slow _____ somewhere near the shore of the lake."

2. Their supplies were _____, and they didn't know how long they would last.

3. They came _____ back after their dramatic flight.

4. Each family was _____ a certain amount of water.

5. They were very _____ as they talked about the lack of edible plant life.

6. It was a _____ designed to sow seeds.

7. Their wings were bright, a dusty silver marked with _____.

8. They discovered the huge boulders in a large valley like an _____.

9. Father's _____ book explained how to make things.

10. Once they were _____, they flew in pairs.

11. "We have just about used up our _____," said Father.

12. We began to understand that they were not _____.

13. They didn't realize how _____ books and stories were.

14. They all tried to _____ a way to cut the trees down.

15. It was a _____ that several of them had brought Robinson Crusoe.

16. The close-packed grains of wheat had edges; they were _____.

Independent Reading Activities That Keep Kids Learning... While You Teach Small Groups • Scholastic Professional Books

Wordplay: It's Pun and Games

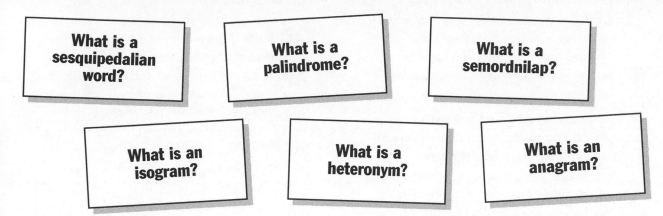

What is a sesquipedalian word?

What is a palindrome?

What is a semordnilap?

What is an isogram?

What is a heteronym?

What is an anagram?

Authors and poets who bring wordplay into the classroom also bring the element of fun. Humor is a powerful motivator, and wordplay offers a kind of enrichment that can't be measured. Picture books, poetry books, chapter books, and novels that incorporate wordplay can get children excited about language and vocabulary. And books featuring wordplay are readily shared in guided reading groups, with the whole class, or as the basis for a center activity or long-term project.

Consider using Roald Dahl's *The BFG* as a read-aloud. Dahl's adroit use of the language—a wonderful conglomeration of puns, spoonerisms, malapropisms, and portmanteau words—makes his Big Friendly Giant a most memorable literary character. And, if you really want some heavy-duty wordplay, read Norton Juster's *The Phantom Tollbooth*. Poets whose innovative play with words will delight your students include Douglas Florian, Jack Prelutsky, Shel Silverstein, Myra Cohn Livingston, Eve Merriam, John Ciardi, Kathleen O'Connell George, among many others.

Here are some definitions and just a few ideas to get you started:

✦ **A sesquipedalian word is a multisyllabic word.** In my classroom, the words we considered "long" had at least four syllables.

We collected them. (Some people collect stuffed animals; this is your opportunity to be different!) Set aside a bulletin board and have students bring in big words. Print them on sentence strips and help your students learn about the syllables. "Sesquipedalian," by the way, is a sesquipedalian word.

✦ **A palindrome is a word that is spelled the same forwards and backwards.** "Hannah" is a palindrome. So are "racecar", "Otto," "Mom," "Dad," and the title of John Agee's book about palindromes, *Sit on a Potato Pan, Otis!* Collect palindromes and you'll be amazed at the number of students who are looking more closely at words.

✦ **If you spell *palindromes* backward, you get the word *semordnilap*.** A semordnilap is a word that, when spelled backwards, makes another word. "Diaper" spelled backwards is "repaid" (how true!) and "drawer" spelled backwards is "reward." ("Drawer" is also a heteronym, discussed below.) Stanley Yelnats, Louis Sacher's hero in the 1999 Newbery Award-winning book, *Holes*, has a palindromic name, but his last name is a semordnilap derived from spelling his first name backwards.

Independent Reading Activities That Keep Kids Learning... While You Teach Small Groups • Scholastic Professional Books

✦ **When you tire of collecting semordnilaps, go for isograms.** Isograms are words in which no letter of the alphabet appears more than once. It is easy to find short isograms, but real word lovers are constantly searching for long isograms. The word *palindrome* is, in fact, an isogram.

✦ **Heteronyms are words that are spelled the same but have different pronunciations and different meanings.** *Bow, row, buffet, conduct, does,* and *dove* are examples of heteronyms. Heteronyms are great collectibles because there are so many. Use heteronyms as a center activity, asking students to put them into sentences. Collecting heteronyms reinforces the use of context clues for determining pronunciation.

✦ **When the letters in a word can be rearranged to make another word, it's an anagram.** One of my favorite anagrams is the word *listen*. Rearranged, the letters also make the word *silent*. Other examples include *seated* and *teased*, *steal* and *tales*, *heart* and *earth*, and *tired* and *tried*. How many students have you encountered who have misspelled *tired* and *tried*? Consider an ongoing anagram search. Once my students discovered anagrams they were constantly moving letters around in words and coming to me with their "discoveries" when they were able to create new words. We called this our "ongoing anagram search"; it continued all year.

The following books are excellent resources for building an appreciation for playing with words:

John Agee
Sit on a Potato Pan, Otis!

John Agee
Who Ordered the Jumbo Shrimp?

John Agee
Elvis Lives! And Other Anagrams

John Agee
Go Hang a Salami, I'm a Lasagna Hog

Andrew Clements
Double Trouble in Walla Walla

Kalli Dakos
Get Out of the Alphabet, Number 2

Cathryn Falwell
Word Wizard

Debra Frasier
Miss Alaineus

Lynda Graham-Barber
A Chartreuse Leotard in a Magenta Limousine

Fred Gwynne
A Little Pigeon Toad

Cathi Hepworth
An Alphabetical Anthology

Patrick J. Lewis
Doodle Dandies: Poems That Take Shape

Bernard Most
Hippopotamus Hunt

Otto Seibold and Vivian Walsh
Olive, the Other Reindeer

William Steig
CDB! and CDC!

Marvin Terban
Funny You Should Ask: How to Make Up Jokes and Riddles with Wordplay

Richard Wilbur
The Disappearing Alphabet

Richard Wilbur
The Pig in the Spigot

For a terrific resource book, consider **Word Circus** by Richard Lederer. Written for adults, it has great ideas that can easily be adapted for the classroom.

Independent Reading Activities That Keep Kids Learning... While You Teach Small Groups • Scholastic Professional Books

Heteronyms: Playing With Words

Name: _____ **Date:** _____

Directions: Heteronyms are words that are spelled the same but pronounced differently. They also have very different meanings. For instance, the word *dove* might refer to a bird, but it could explain how someone went into the swimming pool as well. Often, we must depend on context—how the word is used—to determine how to pronounce it. Used one way, the word may be a noun; used another way, it could be a verb.

Below are ten sets of heteronyms. Use the dictionary to find and write a different definition for each of the two heteronyms in a set. On another sheet of paper, write a sentence for each of the different meanings of the words. Attach that sheet to this page.

minute	
minute	

desert	
desert	

bow	
bow	

close	
close	

Independent Reading Activities That Keep Kids Learning... While You Teach Small Groups • Scholastic Professional Books

object	
object	

record	
record	

contest	
contest	

refuse	
refuse	

tear	
tear	

wind	
wind	

Independent Reading Activities That Keep Kids Learning... While You Teach Small Groups • Scholastic Professional Books

Poetry for Different Purposes

> *When you give a child poems (remembering, once the silence closes back over the end of the poem, not to ask "what does this mean?" but rather, "what did you feel?" or "what did you see?"), you are opening up different parts of his or her reading apparatus than fiction or drama or journalism open up.*
>
> — Jorie Graham

Teaching students to use different models of poetry is an excellent way to help them feel comfortable writing their own poems. Children can use poetry to summarize a field trip, a videotape, the visit of a guest speaker, or a special assembly. They can write poetry at a center or as part of a long-term never-ending project. They can report on a book, synthesize content information, or bring closure to a unit of study, all through poetry. The types of poetry listed below—some old and some new—are easily taught, easily mastered, and very versatile.

✦ List Poems
A list poem may be a single column of words generated about a topic or a series of phrases that are a response to a prompt. Begin by brainstorming: Ask students to write down everything they can think of about a specific topic. (It's best if the topic is something students care about; this makes the brainstorming more energetic.)

List the words on the chalkboard and then allow each student to choose words to create a list poem of his or her own. The first word on the list should name the topic and the last word on the list can be a synonym for the topic, a word that provides closure, or simply a repeat of the first word.

✦ Group Poems
These are great for summing up a unit of study. Each student contributes a line of poetry, and students work together to decide on the sequence of the lines. Groups may be assigned to report on different parts of a chapter, the results of a science experiment, or a visit by a guest speaker. Final editing can be done by the whole class or in small groups.

✦ Two-Word Poems
The rule here is simple: two words, two words, two words, and so on. They are read across the page, they don't have to rhyme, and they subtly build summarizing skills. Here is one example, from third-graders who summarized a fable this way:

Cat	moved
into	house.
Mice	became
very	scared.
One	mouse
said	to
bell	the
cat.	Who
will	do
that?	asked
the	wise
old	mouse.

✦ Partner Poetry
In partner poetry, two students work together to create two-word poems. The poems can be written as responses (to a book or a performance, for instance) and then dramatized.

Independent Reading Activities That Keep Kids Learning... While You Teach Small Groups • Scholastic Professional Books

✦ Telephone and Address Poems

The children write their telephone numbers vertically along the left-hand side of the page. Each number indicates the number of words to be written in each line. A zero in the phone number means 10 words. For address poems, the student lists vertically the numbers of his or her street address and follows the same procedure as for telephone poems. The student then writes vertically the letters of the street name and begins a new line of the poem with each letter.

✦ Pyramid Poems

The format is very simple. Just one word in line one, two words in line two, three words in line three, and so on—to the eighth line, which will have eight words. Pyramid poems are wonderful for teaching summarizing skills.

✦ Copycat Poems

One of my favorites! Find a poem you admire and have students mimic the poet's rhyme patterns, form, mood, or structure. Plan on this activity taking some time, as students must first develop something to say about a topic, and then experiment with the phrasing in order to match the model. Copycat poems are especially successful when students already have a good deal of meaningful content that they want to write about.

✦ Bio-Poem

They've been around a long time, but haven't outlived their usefulness. Here's the format:

Line One:	Character's name
Line Two:	Four words that describe him/her
Line Three:	Five words that are identifiers—tells who or what the character is
Line Four:	Lover of (name three things)
Line Five:	Who feels (name three emotions)
Line Six:	Who needs (name three things)
Line Seven:	Who gives (name three things)
Line Eight:	Who fears (name three things)
Line Nine:	Who likes to wear (name three things)
Line Ten:	Who would like to see (finish this sentence)
Line Eleven:	Lives (give information about geographic location)
Line Twelve:	Repeat Line One

Bio-poems can be used for book reports, biography reports, and autobiographical sketches. With slight changes, they can be used to describe inanimate objects. I've also had my students write autobiographical versions, using newly learned character trait adjectives for line two.

✦ Mask Poems*

I first discovered this poetry format on the Web site of the wonderful poet, Kristine O'Connell George (www.kristinegeorge.com). In a nutshell, a mask poem speaks to the reader in a different "voice" or point of view. Rather than having an observer comment on a tree, for instance, the tree comments on itself. George says, "Children enjoy pretending to be something else and intuitively understand seeing their world in this way…"

For more detailed information about mask poems, go to the Web site above, click on "For Teachers," go to "*Old Elm Speaks*," and scroll down to "Tree Voices"—*Writing Exercises*. The site has many links to other poetry resources and an abundance of ideas for teaching students about poetry.

"A Street Tree" from *Old Elm Speaks* (Clarion Books, 1998) is an excellent mask poem to read aloud with students. You can use it as a point of departure for a discussion about mask poems, focusing on who is speaking and who is being spoken to, as well as for inspiration for children's own poems. Mask poems can also be used with science or social studies content.

To help students imagine who or what they might like to pretend to be, George suggests asking students questions like the following:

- *What is your day like?*
- *What do you see? Feel? Hear? Smell?*
- *What makes you happy or afraid?*
- *What do you dream about?*

*This information is © www.kristinegeorge.com and used with permission.

CHAPTER 7

Easy Long-Term Never-Ending Projects

Have you ever noticed how difficult it is to teach a group when a child is tugging on your sleeve saying, "Teacher, I'm finished. What do I do now?" Well, I've solved that problem. I've invented something they can't finish—at least not very quickly. Each of these long-term never-ending projects is designed to last anywhere from four to eight weeks or longer. And be sure to introduce them as "never-ending;" your students should truly think they will never end. The projects themselves are varied and include activities like using picture books in pre-writing strategies, Dewey Decimal studies, author-focused activities, and many more.

All work should be kept in manila folders. To help students practice responsibility—and avoid losing papers—hole-punch the folders and give students brads to hold their work inside. It's a good idea to adapt a rubric to fit the project so students can set goals for themselves. Monitor these projects on an ongoing basis by periodically asking children to bring up their folders when you meet with them individually or in small groups. At the end of the project (because of course there actually is an end!), collect the folders and correct and comment on/grade the work as promptly as possible.

At the point when you've decided that it's time to move on, simply announce, "Boys and girls, believe it or not, our long-term never-ending project is ending on Friday. So, we'll start a new long-term never-ending project on Monday." My students were always eager to begin the next long-term project. Not knowing exactly when the project would end added to their interest. This chapter offers almost two dozen project ideas that should help you keep your students learning if not forever, then for a very long time.

 Picture Books All Over the Place: A Bibliography is a listing of more than two dozen picture books ranging from second to sixth grade in readability, chosen specifically because place is important within the stories.

 Picture Books All Over The Place: A Comparison Table provides a matrix for recording the results of an investigation. (The investigation is based on the picture books in the preceding bibliography.) For each book, students check off the categories that apply.

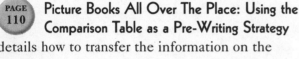 **Picture Books All Over The Place: Using the Comparison Table as a Pre-Writing Strategy** details how to transfer the information on the matrix into a five-paragraph report. Students use the matrix as a graphic organizer and as the basis for a writing assignment, thus working through the process of turning discrete factual information into a structured report.

 The Long-Term Never-Ending Picture Book Project for Older Readers is a bibliography of thought-provoking titles designed to involve intermediate students.

 Projects for "The Long-Term Never-Ending Picture Book Project" works in tandem with the preceding bibliography. Students complete a different project from a menu on this page for each picture book read

Chapter-Book Check-Off is appropriate for students just beginning to read chapter books. Because this project focuses on series books, it's a great way to get your students hooked on an author. To adjust for differences in your classroom, you may have two different long-term never-ending projects in place at the same time.

The Phoenix: A Never-Ending Bird lists books that have won the Phoenix Award—an award given to books that have never won a prize. Like the mythical phoenix, these books have risen from the ashes to receive deserved recognition. This project is more appropriate for older, fluent readers. Some of my personal favorites are here. Recognize any of yours?

The Phoenix Matrix: A Never-Ending Project is based on the bibliography on the previous page. This matrix invites students to check off different categories if they apply to a particular book read. Students must also write a paragraph for each book using information extrapolated from the matrix.

Books About Books crosses genres and reading levels. There's something here for everybody. The unifying aspect is that every book listed tells a story that involves books. This long-term never-ending project would also be an excellent literature study for a small group of students.

It's a Numbers Game revisits the Dewey side of the library. Students total the numbers in the Dewey Decimal Number of a particular book and add ten to determine how many words they will include in a brief summary of the book. It is easy to individualize with this long-term never-ending project because struggling readers will be able to find books they can read for most of the topics, while your more able readers will be able to choose more challenging books.

Waiting for the Next Harry Potter is my idea of a great long-term never-ending project, especially since I love fantasies. Students select a row on a grid and read the five fantasy books in that row. For more able readers, this can become a genre study as well.

Choices and Options provides a menu of possible activities, each of which results in a different original student product. The activities are based on the books read in the fantasy book grid on the preceding page.

PAGE 121 **Fantasies: A Long-Term Never-Ending Project** is a matrix for the bonus option on the previous page, but it is also a page that stands alone. Any titles will work on the matrix. For instance, there are many fantasies written for children just transitioning to chapter books. *Knights of the Kitchen Table*, part of *The Time Warp Trio* books by Jon Scieszka is but one example. The features of a fantasy will certainly be familiar to Harry Potter fans, so this matrix will need little explanation. (Many thanks to J.K. Rowling for making our jobs easier.)

PAGE 122 **Notable Nonfiction Authors** again sends children to the Dewey side of the library. This page, a chart of nonfiction author names, directs students to look each author up in the library or on the computer, write down the Dewey Decimal Number of a book that looks interesting, and then read that book.

PAGE 123 **Nonfiction Assignment Options** is a list of projects based on the nonfiction books students have selected on the previous page. You can adjust the difficulty level of this assignment easily by requiring a different number of books to be read. For struggling readers, perhaps four or five would be the maximum. To challenge more able readers, require more books to be read and focus on authors who write books with greater concept density. Although most of the options on this page are quite serious, one amuses me greatly: "Even if you thought your book was really boring, work very hard and come up with five good things to say about it!"

PAGE 124 **The Long-Term Never-Ending "Choose an Author" Project** is another way to get students hooked on an author. There is something quite wonderful about a child who can talk in a literate fashion about a favorite author, and this project may just begin that attachment. Books are available from these authors for children reading

from third-grade level to eighth-grade level, and just about every genre one can think of is represented in their writings.

PAGE 125 **Activities for the Long-Term Never-Ending "Choose an Author" Project** invites students to select a different activity from a menu of ten choices for each book they've read by an author listed on the previous page.

PAGE 126 **There's Fiction in the System** investigates this anomaly: Why is some fiction shelved on the nonfiction side of the library? What was Dewey thinking? This long-term never-ending project guides your students to folk tales, fairytales, riddles, poetry, and plays. Don't tell them where they're going, just let them discover Dewey's mysterious ways. (Dewey gave most fictional literature the number 813, but because there are so many books of this type, libraries house them separately. The genres named above still retain their original Dewey numbers and libraries still classify them that way. Interesting, isn't it?)

PAGE 127 **The Long-Term Never-Ending Series Project** asks students to read two to three books by six different series authors. This is a great way for children to get immersed in a particular character and really get to know him or her. These authors have written books about specific characters that are most appropriate for readers at second- and third-grade reading levels. Some will also work with fourth grade. Because of their interest factor, books that will work with older struggling readers include those by John R. Erickson, Gertrude Warner, and Beverly Cleary.

PAGE 128 **Characters in Series Books: Getting to Know Them** puts to use the knowledge students have gained by reading multiple books about one character. This activity asks readers to identify character traits and then write brief character descriptions based on the lists.

Picture Books All Over the Place: A Bibliography

Directions: Stories happen in all kinds of places. *Where* they happen usually influences *what* happens. Read nine picture books. At least five should be from this list. The other four also can be from this list or they may be any other picture books that appeal to you. Fill in the chart on the next page after you read each book.

Becky Bloom
Wolf!

Rosemary Breckler
Sweet Dried Apples:
A Vietnamese Wartime Childhood

Don Brown
Alice Ramsey's Grand Adventure

Eve Bunting
Your Move

Lynne Cherry
The Great Kapok Tree

Barbara Cooney
Island Boy

Joy Cowley
The Video Shop Sparrow

Donald Crews
Bigmama's

Paul Fleischman
Weslandia

Virginia Hamilton
Jaguarundi

Ronald Himmler
Rudi's Pond

Will Hobbs
Howling Hill

James Howe
Horace and Morris
But Mostly Dolores

Thomas Locker
The Land of Gray Wolf

Megan McDonald
The Bone Keeper

Megan McDonald
The Night Iguana Left Home

David McPhail
Mole Music

Herman Melville
Catskill Eagle

Pam Muñoz Ryan
Amelia and Eleanor
Go for a Ride

Christopher Myers
Black Cat

Jerdine Nolen
Raising Dragons

Robert Priest
The Old Pirate of
Central Park

Laurence Pringle
One Room School

Tres Seymour
Jake Johnson,
The Story of a Mule

Judy Sierra
Tasty Baby Belly Buttons

Michael Tunnell
Mailing May

Frances Weller
Madaket Millie

David Wiesner
Sector 7

Independent Reading Activities That Keep Kids Learning… While You Teach Small Groups • Scholastic Professional Books

Picture Books All Over the Place: A Comparison Table

Name: _____

Date: _____

Directions: On the chart, write the title of each picture book that you have read. Check off all appropriate boxes for each book.

Book Title	The story took place in an unusual setting.	Both illustrator and author were absolutely necessary to tell the story.	The illustrations were more important than the words.	The illustrations were not as important as the words were.	Where the story happened is why the story happened.
1.					
2.					
3.					
4.					
5.					
6.					
7.					
8.					
9.					

Independent Reading Activities That Keep Kids Learning... While You Teach Small Groups • Scholastic Professional Books

Picture Books All Over the Place:
Using the Comparison Table as a Pre-Writing Strategy

Name: _____ **Date:** _____

Directions: The information that you gathered on the comparison table on page 109 can be used as the basis for a five-paragraph report about picture books. Each of the table categories will become the topic of a paragraph. The directions below describe how to write each paragraph. Use a separate sheet of paper for your report; attach it to this page.

First paragraph: Name all the books that took place in an unusual setting. Think about the settings. Use this format:

Several of the books that I read took place in an unusual setting. (*Write title of book here*) took place in (*write where it took place here*). (*Continue writing sentences with titles and settings until you have named all the titles that fit this category.*)

Second paragraph: Name all the books that needed both the author and the illustrator to tell the story. The second paragraph will look like this:

I think the author and the illustrator were both needed in _____, _____, and _____. (*Write the titles of any books that fit this category.*)

Third paragraph: Name all the books in which illustrations were more important than the words. The third paragraph will look like this:

The illustrations in _____, _____, and _____ were more important than the words. The illustrator showed _____. (*Explain how the illustrations were more important than the words.*)

Fourth paragraph: Using the same format as above, write about books in which the words were definitely more important than the illustrations.

The words in _____, _____, and _____ were more important than the illustrations. The author's words were more important than the illustrations because _____. (*Explain why the words were more important.*)

Fifth paragraph: In this paragraph, name each book that fits in the last category and describe why that particular setting was really needed for this story to even take place.

In _____ (*name book*), the story *needed* to take place in the _____ (*describe the setting*) because _____. (*Tell how the setting was critically important to the story.*)

Independent Reading Activities That Keep Kids Learning... While You Teach Small Groups • Scholastic Professional Books

The Long-Term Never-Ending Picture Book Project for Older Readers

Directions: Beware! Reading the following picture books may require you to think. Read a book from the chart below. Then complete one of the assignment options from the list of projects on the next page. Repeat this at least seven times, reading seven (or more) books and selecting a different assignment for each book until all options have been completed at least once.

The Watertower by Gary Crew	**Sister Anne's Hands** by Marybeth Lorbiecki	**Stone Girl, Bone Girl** by Laurence Anholt
Black and White by David Macaulay	**Night Golf** by William Miller	**Home Run** by Robert Burleigh
Mysterious Thelonious by Christopher Raschka	**An Angel for Solomon Singer** by Cynthia Rylant	**Smoky Night** by David Diaz
Tibet: Through the Red Box by Peter Sis	**Wilma Unlimited** by Kathleen Krull	**The Cello of Mr. O** by Jane Cutler
The Flying Latke by Arthur Yorkinks	**Duke Ellington** by Andrea Davis Pinkney	**The Bobbin Girl** by Emily Arnold McCully
Voices in the Park by Anthony Browne	**Starry Messenger** by Peter Sis	**The Whispering Cloth** by Pegi Deitz Shea
Zoom by Istvan Banyai	**Fly Away Home** by Eve Bunting	**Molly Bannaky** by Alice McGill
I, Crocodile by Fred Marcellino	**I Have Heard of a Land** by Joyce Carol Thomas	**The Wretched Stone** by Chris Van Allsburg

Independent Reading Activities That Keep Kids Learning... While You Teach Small Groups • Scholastic Professional Books

Projects for "The Long-Term Never-Ending Picture Book Project"

Name: _____ **Date:** _____

Directions: After you have read one of the picture books for older readers from the list on page 111, choose one of the projects below. Select a different activity for each book until you have done each activity at least once. When your completed project has been approved, put an X in the appropriate square below.

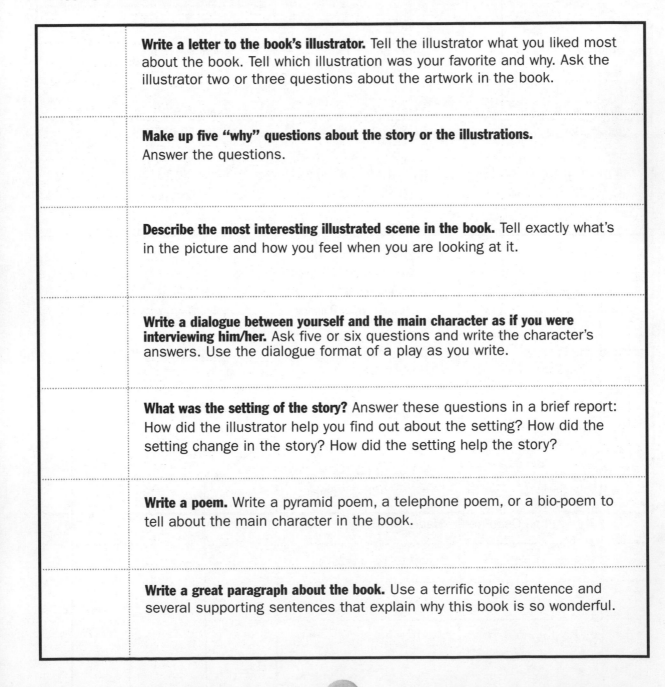

Write a letter to the book's illustrator. Tell the illustrator what you liked most about the book. Tell which illustration was your favorite and why. Ask the illustrator two or three questions about the artwork in the book.

Make up five "why" questions about the story or the illustrations. Answer the questions.

Describe the most interesting illustrated scene in the book. Tell exactly what's in the picture and how you feel when you are looking at it.

Write a dialogue between yourself and the main character as if you were interviewing him/her. Ask five or six questions and write the character's answers. Use the dialogue format of a play as you write.

What was the setting of the story? Answer these questions in a brief report: How did the illustrator help you find out about the setting? How did the setting change in the story? How did the setting help the story?

Write a poem. Write a pyramid poem, a telephone poem, or a bio-poem to tell about the main character in the book.

Write a great paragraph about the book. Use a terrific topic sentence and several supporting sentences that explain why this book is so wonderful.

Independent Reading Activities That Keep Kids Learning... While You Teach Small Groups • Scholastic Professional Books

Chapter-Book Check-Off

Name: _____ **Date:** _____

Pre-Reading Directions: Some authors write many books about the same characters. These are called series books. The books listed below are all series books. Choose one series and read a book in that series. Put a check mark in the left-hand column and write the title of that book in the far right column. If you'd like to read another book in that series, add the author, series, and title to the bottom of the list and check it off after you've read it. Then follow the *After-Reading Directions* at the bottom of the next page (page 114).

✔	Author	Series	Book Title
	David Adler	*Cam Jansen mysteries*	
	Stan Berenstain	*Berenstain Bears books*	
	Eth Clifford	*Flatfoot Fox books*	
	Debbie Dadey	*Bailey School Kids books*	
	John R. Erickson	*Hank the Cowdog books*	
	Paula Danziger	*Amber Brown books*	
	Patricia Reilly Giff	*Polk Street School books*	
	Dan Greenburg	*Zack books*	
	Russell Hoban	*Frances books*	
	James Howe	*Pinky and Rex books*	
	Suzy Kline	*Horrible Harry books*	
	Arnold Lobel	*Frog and Toad books*	
	Mary Pope Osborne	*Magic Tree House books*	
	Barbara Park	*Junie B. Jones books*	
	Peggy Parish	*Amelia Bedelia books*	
	John Peterson	*The Littles books*	

Independent Reading Activities That Keep Kids Learning... While You Teach Small Groups • Scholastic Professional Books

✔	Author	Series	Book Title
	Ron Roy	*A to Z Mystery books*	
	Cynthia Rylant	*Poppleton books*	
	Louis Sachar	*Marvin Redpost books*	
	Jon Scieszka	*Time Warp Trio books*	
	Marjorie Sharmat	*Nate the Great books*	
	Donald J. Sobol	*Encyclopedia Brown books*	
	Jean Van Leeuwen	*Amanda Pig books*	
	Gertrude Warner	*Boxcar Children books*	

After-Reading Directions: For each book that you read (including those you've added), do Activity A or Activity B. Use a separate sheet of paper for your work; attach it to this page.

Activity A:
1. Make up two questions about your book that begin with the word "where."
2. Make up two questions about your book that begin with the word "when."
3. Make up two questions about your book that begin with the word "what."
4. Answer each of your questions in complete sentences.

Activity B:
1. Make up two questions about your book that begin with the word "why."
2. Make up two questions about your book that begin with the word "who."
3. Make up two questions about your book that begin with the word "how."
4. Answer each of your questions in complete sentences.

Don't forget to end each question with a question mark.

Independent Reading Activities That Keep Kids Learning... While You Teach Small Groups • Scholastic Professional Books

The Phoenix:
A Never-Ending Bird

Name: _____ **Date:** _____

Directions: The phoenix is a mythical bird that rose from ashes to begin its life again. The Phoenix Award was named after this bird because it is given to a book that also has "risen from the ashes"—one that has never won a prize before. Each year, The Children's Literature Association looks back at excellent literature published twenty years before and invites us to bring it to life again. They believe that there are some books that are just too good to be forgotten. Below is a list of Phoenix Award-winning books. Read as many of these books as you want; think about why the book was given this important award. Check off each book you read, then fill in the matrix on the next page.

☐ **The Seventh Raven**
by Peter Dickinson

☐ **The Night Journey**
by Kathryn Lasky

☐ **The Keeper of the Isis Light**
by Monica Hughes

☐ **Throwing Shadows**
by E. L. Konigsburg

☐ **A Chance Child**
by Jill Paton Walsh

☐ **Beauty**
by Robin McKinley

☐ **The Devil in Vienna**
by Doris Orgel

☐ **The Mark of the Horse Lord**
by Rosemary Sutcliff

☐ **Queenie Peavy**
by Robert Burch

☐ **The Rider and His Horse**
by Erik Christian Haugaard

☐ **The Night Watchmen**
by Helen Cresswell

☐ **Enchantress from the Stars**
by Sylvia Louise Engdahl

☐ **A Long Way from Verona**
by Jane Gardam

☐ **A Sound of Chariots**
by Mollie Hunter

☐ **Carrie's War**
by Nina Bawden

☐ **Of Nightingales That Weep**
by Katherine Paterson

☐ **Dragonwings**
by Laurence Yep

☐ **The Stone Book**
by Alan Garner

☐ **I Am the Cheese**
by Robert Cormier

☐ **Sing Down the Moon**
by Scott O'Dell

☐ **The Tombs of Atuan**
by Ursula Le Guin

☐ **My Brother Sam is Dead**
by James and Christopher Collier

☐ **Listen for the Fig Tree**
by Sharon Bell Mathis

☐ **Tuck Everlasting**
by Natalie Babbitt

☐ **Abel's Island**
by William Steig

Independent Reading Activities That Keep Kids Learning…While You Teach Small Groups • Scholastic Professional Books

The Phoenix Matrix: A Never-Ending Project

Name: _____ **Date:** _____

Directions: Write the title of each Phoenix Award-winning book you read. If, in your opinion, the numbered statement below the chart is true of that book, put a check in the column with the corresponding number. If it is not true, leave the column blank for that book. Then, for each book, write one paragraph about the two categories that are most interesting to you.

Book Title	1	2	3	4	5	6	7

1. There is a remarkable scene in this book that I can't forget.
2. The protagonist has character traits that I really admire.
3. I have some friends who would really like this book.
4. The author uses dialogue among the characters to let us get to know them.
5. The author has an amazing vocabulary, and I learned some new words.
6. There are <u>several</u> characters in this book who are important to the plot.
7. I feel that the author is trying to make an important point that the reader needs to recognize or to learn.

Independent Reading Activities That Keep Kids Learning… While You Teach Small Groups • Scholastic Professional Books

Books About Books

Name: _____

Date: _____

Directions: All of the books on the shelf below are worth reading and all of them focus in some way on the subject of "books." Choose three of them to read, including at least one by an author you have never read. Circle your choices. After reading each book, on another sheet of paper, number three lines and write three reasons why you would (or would not) recommend the book to a friend. Then, in one paragraph, explain the role books played in the story and how books were important to the plot or the characters. Attach the paper to this page.

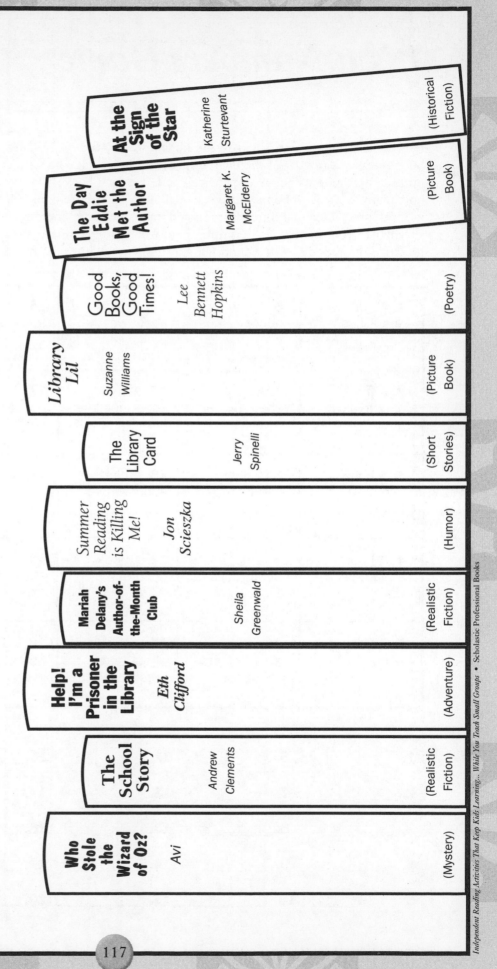

At the Sign of the Star — Katherine Sturtevant (Historical Fiction)

The Day Eddie Met the Author — Margaret K. McElderry (Picture Book)

Good Books, Good Times! — Lee Bennett Hopkins (Poetry)

Library Lil — Suzanne Williams (Picture Book)

The Library Card — Jerry Spinelli (Short Stories)

Summer Reading is Killing Me! — Jon Scieszka (Humor)

Mariah Delany's Author-of-the-Month Club — Sheila Greenwald (Realistic Fiction)

Help! I'm a Prisoner in the Library — Eth Clifford (Adventure)

The School Story — Andrew Clements (Realistic Fiction)

Who Stole the Wizard of Oz? — Avi (Mystery)

Independent Reading Activities That Keep Kids Learning...While You Teach Small Groups • Scholastic Professional Books

It's a Numbers Game

Name: _____ **Date:** _____

Directions: Non-fiction books in the library are shelved using Dewey Decimal numbers. Read a book in every category of the chart and, as you finish each book, record its Dewey Decimal number on the lines below the chart. Then, use each book's Dewey Decimal number to dictate how many words will be in your very brief summary of the book. Here's how: add up the numbers in the Dewey Decimal number, then add ten to that sum and, on a separate sheet of paper, summarize your book with that number of words. For example, for a book with the Dewey Decimal number 299, you would write a summary of 30 words ($2 + 9 + 9 = 20$; $20 + 10 = 30$).

1. A book about flags	**6.** A book about games	**11.** A book about weather	**16.** A book about Japan	**21.** A book about baseball
2. A book about volcanoes	**7.** A book about Benjamin Franklin	**12.** A book about holidays	**17.** A book about national parks	**22.** A book about the solar system
3. A book about Mt. Everest	**8.** A book about ships	**13.** A book about airplanes	**18.** A book about insects	**23.** A book about Africa
4. A book about space travel	**9.** A book about dogs	**14.** A book about Asia	**19.** A book about science experiments	**24.** A book about origami
5. A book about reptiles	**10.** A book about plants	**15.** A book about endangered species	**20.** A book about inventors	**25.** A book about pets

1. _____   6. _____   11. _____   16. _____   21. _____

2. _____   7. _____   12. _____   17. _____   22. _____

3. _____   8. _____   13. _____   18. _____   23. _____

4. _____   9. _____   14. _____   19. _____   24. _____

5. _____   10. _____   15. _____   20. _____   25. _____

Waiting for the Next Harry Potter

Name: _____ **Date:** _____

Directions: If you've finished all the Harry Potter books and you're twiddling your thumbs waiting for the next one, here are some award-winning titles that can take you to other fantasy worlds. Choose a row of books (horizontal, vertical, or diagonal). For each book that you read, choose a different activity from the choices on the next page (page 120) and follow those directions. When you have finished reading a book and your activity has been completed and approved, draw an "X" through the square.

Aria of the Sea by Dia Calhoun	**Night Flying** by Rita Murphy	**Beast** by Donna Jo Napoli	**Growing Wings** by Laurel Winter	**Boots and the Seven Leaguers** by Jane Yolen
Jeremy Thatcher, Dragon Hatcher by Bruce Coville	**Castle in the Air** by Diana Wynne Jones	**Elsewhere** by Will Shetterly	**Song of the Gargoyle** by Zilpha Keatley Snyder	**Knight's Wyrd** by Debra Doyle and James D. Macdonald
Hobkin by Peni R. Griffin	**Jennifer Murdley's Toad** by Bruce Coville	**Fish Soup** by Ursula K. Le Guin	**The Kingdom of Kevin Malone** by Suzy McKee Charnas	**Rose Daughter** by Robin McKinley
Nevernever by Will Shetterly	**Calling on Dragons** by Patricia C. Wrede	**Owl in Love** by Patrice Kindl	**Switching Well** by Peni R. Griffin	**Good Griselle** by Jane Yolen
The Crown of Dalemark by Diana Wynne Jones	**Falcon's Egg** by Luli Gray	**Wren's War** by Sherwood Smith	**Ella Enchanted** by Gail Carson Levine	**The Folk Keeper** by Franny Billingsly

Independent Reading Activities That Keep Kids Learning... While You Teach Small Groups • Scholastic Professional Books

Choices and Options

Name: _____ **Date:** _____

Directions: For each book that you read from the chart on page 119, choose an activity below. Use a separate sheet of paper for the activity and attach it to this page.

Compare yourself to the main character. Share similarities and differences. Use a "We/Me" format. Divide a sheet of paper in half. Label one half the "We" column and list all the ways that you are like the main character. The other half is the "Me" column where you'll list all the ways in which you are different. Write at least two paragraphs summarizing your findings.

Write telephone poems about different characters in the book. Choose three or four of the most important characters. Use your telephone number or a friend's. Each digit dictates the number of words in that line of the poem (e.g., if your phone number is 738-2234, the first line of your poem has seven words, the next line has three words, the third line has eight words, and so on. If there is a zero in your phone number, that line in your poem should have ten words.) The lines in the poem don't have to rhyme or be complete sentences.

Write the title of the book as an acrostic. Summarize your book by using each letter to begin a sentence about the book.

Example: F _____

I _____

S _____

H _____

Find a passage from this book that you'd like to read aloud to your class. Share the title of the book and the author's name. Briefly summarize the book, but don't tell the ending! Practice the passage so that you can read it fluently and with expression. (If there is dialogue in the passage, you may choose to use different voices for the different characters.) With your teacher, plan a time for your performance.

Create ten questions about your book. Think about the words that are most often used to write questions. Five words that commonly begin a question include: who, what, where, when and why. Write two questions that begin with the word "What," two questions that begin with the word "When," two questions that begin with the word "Who," two questions that begin with the word "Where," and two questions that begin with the word "Why." Then, using complete sentences, answer each question.

BONUS: After you've read all five books, do a feature analysis. Use the matrix on page 121 and follow those directions to analyze the fantasy genre.

Independent Reading Activities That Keep Kids Learning... While You Teach Small Groups • Scholastic Professional Books

Fantasies: A Long-Term Never-Ending Project

Name: _____

Date: _____

Directions: Use this matrix to do a feature analysis of five different fantasy books. As you read, put checks in the appropriate columns for each book. Notice that most fantasies do have some elements in common. Look for elements that are different as well. After completing the matrix, summarize your findings in a three or four paragraph report.

Title of Fantasy	Spells or talismans	Humor	Supernatural creatures	Superstitions	Good vs. Evil	Invented world	Time constraints	Invisibility

Independent Reading Activities That Keep Kids Learning... While You Teach Small Groups • Scholastic Professional Books

Notable Nonfiction Authors

Name: _____   **Date:** _____

Directions: To locate a nonfiction book by one of these authors, look up the author's last name on the computer or in the card catalog in your library. When you find a book that looks interesting, write its Dewey Decimal number in the corresponding author's square below. After you have read the book, choose one assignment option on the next page. Put an "X" in the square when your finished assignment has been approved.

Seymour Simon	Kathleen Krull	Jerry Pallotta	Andrew Langley	Jerry Stanley
Diane Stanley	Diane Hoyt-Goldsmith	James Cross Giblin	Virginia Wright-Frierson	Penny Colman
Mitsumasa Anno	Meredith Hooper	Jim Brandenburg	Lynne Cherry	Russell Freedman
Mary E. Lyons	Linda Lowery	Bruce McMillan	Jacqueline Briggs Martin	Lois Ehlert
Jim Murphy	Anne Rockwell	George Sullivan	Bo Zounders	Margy Burns Knight
Kate Waters	Gare Thompson	Terry Egan, Stan Friedman & Mike Levine	Sylvia Branzei	Kathryn Lasky
Jim Arnosky	Wendy Pfeffer	Robert Ballard	Gail Gibbons	Milton Meltzer
Joanna Cole	Tana Hoban	Scott Steedman	Jean Fritz	Patricia Lauber

Independent Reading Activities That Keep Kids Learning... While You Teach Small Groups • Scholastic Professional Books

Nonfiction Assignment Options

Name: _____ **Date:** _____

Directions: When you finish a nonfiction book by an author listed in the chart on page 122, select one of the assignment options below. For each book, choose a different assignment. Put your initials in the space to show which assignments you have completed. Do your work on a separate sheet of paper and attach it to this page

Initials

	Write a paragraph that follows this pattern: • *First sentence:* Before I read about this topic, I thought that… • *Second sentence:* But when I read about it, I found out that… • *Third sentence:* I also learned that… • *Fourth sentence:* Furthermore, I learned that… • *Fifth sentence:* Finally, I found out that… • *Sixth sentence:* In my opinion, this book is…
	Using new vocabulary words from the book, create a crossword puzzle. Put at least 20 words into your puzzle. Make up clues that are definitions for the words.
	Write two paragraphs, one for each of these questions: (1) Was this book interesting or was it boring? Explain your opinion. (2) If you had written this book, what would you have done to make it more interesting? Give at least three substantial suggestions.
	What did you learn? Write ten facts about the topic of your book.
	Create a survey designed to find out how much people know about the subject of your book. Make up ten questions to ask at least ten people. Show the results of your survey on a graph.
	Even if you thought your book was really boring, work very hard and come up with five good things to say about it.
	Did the title of your book spark your interest? Did the title fit the book? Write a paragraph to explain why or why not. Then make up five titles that would be just as good or even better for the book. Use a thesaurus if you'd like.

Independent Reading Activities That Keep Kids Learning… While You Teach Small Groups • Scholastic Professional Books

The Long-Term Never-Ending "Choose an Author" Project

Name: _____ **Date:** _____

Directions: Each of the following authors has written several chapter books. Select and check off the name of one author. Read five different books that he or she has written. Write the titles of the books below. For each of the books, complete one of the activities on the next page.

☐ **Dick King-Smith**   ☐ **Jean Fritz**   ☐ **Roald Dahl**

☐ **Bruce Coville**   ☐ **Matt Christopher**   ☐ **Avi**

☐ **Betsy Byars**   ☐ **Willo Davis**   ☐ **Phyllis Reynolds**
                             Roberts   **Naylor**

☐ **Peg Kehret**   ☐ **Jon Scieszka**   ☐ **Louis Sachar**

I read these books:

1. _____

2. _____

3. _____

4. _____

5. _____

Independent Reading Activities That Keep Kids Learning... While You Teach Small Groups • Scholastic Professional Books

Activities for the Long-Term Never-Ending "Choose an Author" Project

Name: _____ **Date:** _____

Directions: Choose a different activity for each book that you read by one of the authors listed on page 124. Complete the activities on a separate sheet of paper and attach it to this page. Once your completed activity has been approved, put a check in the box.

❑ Make up ten 5-W questions (Who? What? When? Where? and Why?) about your book. Using complete sentences, answer your questions.

❑ Write a telephone poem about each of the main characters in your book. Directions for writing a telephone poem are on page 120.

❑ Create a crossword puzzle. The words in the puzzle should be one-word answers to questions about the book. The questions are the clues.

❑ Write a pyramid poem to summarize your book.*

❑ Do a We/Me comparison of you and the main character. Directions for making a We/Me comparison are on page 120.

❑ Write a two- or three-sentence summary of each of the chapters in the book you selected.

❑ Use the Internet to locate information about the author whose books you've read. Make up twenty questions about the author. Each question should be able to be answered by one fact from the information you found.

❑ Prepare an oral presentation. Choose an excerpt from your book and practice reading it aloud. Introduce the scene to your class and explain its importance within the story. Be sure to rehearse.

❑ Write your own Readers' Theater version of one of the chapters in your book. Present it to the class. (You may have a friend perform it with you.)

*Note to the teacher: Directions for constructing pyramid poems are on page 104.

Independent Reading Activities That Keep Kids Learning... While You Teach Small Groups • Scholastic Professional Books

There's Fiction in the System

Name: _____   Date: _____

Directions: The Dewey Decimal numbering system helps us primarily in classifying and locating nonfiction. But folk tales, fairy tales, riddles, poetry, and plays are all examples of *fiction* that you'll find classified under their Dewey Decimal numbers in the library. When Melvil Dewey invented the system, he assigned numbers to *all* books, not just nonfiction. He gave most fictional literature the number 813. However, there are so many books of this type that libraries usually have a separate place to house them—the fiction part of the library. They are not numbered but instead are shelved alphabetically by the authors' last names. To investigate the way Dewey numbered other books that are not nonfiction, read two books in each of the numbered categories below. Write their titles in the appropriate space.

812	
811	
398.6	
398.2	
398	

The Long-Term Never-Ending Series Project

Directions: Each of the authors named below has written several books about the same main character. Books by the same author about the same character are called "series books." Read at least six books by different authors below. Then complete the "Characters in Series Books: Getting to Know Them" activity on page 128.

David Adler writes books about Cam Jansen	**Barbara Park** writes books about Junie B. Jones	**Peggy Parish** writes books about Amelia Bedelia	**John R. Erickson** writes books about Hank the Cowdog
Russell Hoban writes books about Frances	**Louis Sachar** writes books about Marvin Redpost	**Eth Clifford** writes books about Flatfoot Fox	**Paula Danziger** writes books about Amber Brown
Arnold Lobel writes books about Frog and Toad	**Suzy Kline** writes books about Horrible Harry	**Gertrude Warner** writes books about the Boxcar Children	**Beverly Cleary** writes books about Ramona Quimby
James Marshall writes books about George and Martha	**Cynthia Rylant** writes books about Henry and Mudge	**Donald J. Sobol** writes books about Encyclopedia Brown	**Marjorie Sharmat** writes books about Nate the Great

Independent Reading Activities That Keep Kids Learning... While You Teach Small Groups • Scholastic Professional Books

Characters in Series Books: Getting to Know Them

Name: _____ **Date:** _____

Directions: One advantage to reading series books is that you really get to know the main characters well. After you have read two or three books about one character from the chart on page 127, write that character's name in the left-hand column. In the right-hand column, write down five character trait words to describe him or her. On a separate sheet of paper, use those character trait words to create five sentences about the character that also tell something about the story. Do this for a total of six different main characters. Attach that sheet to this page.

Character	Character Traits

Independent Reading Activities That Keep Kids Learning While You Teach Small Groups • Scholastic Professional Books